The Study and Criticism of Italian Art

THE STUDY AND CRITICISM OF ITALIAN ART

THIRD SERIES

BY THE SAME AUTHOR.

THE STUDY AND CRITICISM OF ITALIAN ART.
FIRST AND SECOND SERIES. Small 4to. With numerous Illustrations. 10s. 6d. *net each*.

FIRST SERIES: Vasari in the Light of Recent Publications—Dante's Visual Images and his Early Illustrators—Venetian Painting—Correggio—Giorgione's Lost Originals—Amico di Sandro. (*Second Edition, revised*).

SECOND SERIES: A Word for Renaissance Churches—Alessio Baldovinetti—The Caen Sposalizio—Certain unrecognized paintings by Masolino—An unpublished Masterpiece by Filippino Lippi—The British Museum "Raphael" Cartoon—An Altar-piece by Girolamo da Cremona—The Drawings of Andrea Mantegna—Rudiments of Connoisseurship.

LONDON: G. BELL AND SONS, LTD.

THE STUDY AND CRITICISM OF
ITALIAN ART

BY

BERNHARD BERENSON

THIRD SERIES

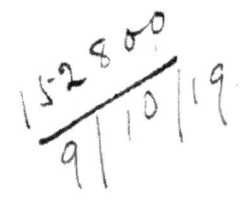

LONDON
G. BELL AND SONS, LTD.
1916

CHISWICK PRESS: CHARLES WHITTINGHAM AND CO
TOOKS COURT, CHANCERY LANE, LONDON.

PREFACE

OF the six essays composing this volume, five are concerned with questions of Venetian Painting in the Fifteenth Century. They have been selected out of a number waiting to appear in book form because they treat of problems or elaborate points for which there was no room in another book, published at the same time under the title of "Venetian Painting in the United States: the Fifteenth Century."

The two, however, on Carpaccio's "Glory of St. Ursula" and on "A Carpacciesque Madonna in Berlin" stand somewhat apart. They are chiefly essays in method, illustrating by example the importance of chronology in our studies.

The paper on Leonardo is an attempt at a revaluation which may interest the general reader.

B. B.

SETTIGNANO,
 1 *September* 1916.

CONTENTS

	PAGE
LEONARDO	1
ST. JUSTINE OF THE BAGATTI VALSECCHI COLLECTION AT MILAN	38
THE FOUR BELLINESQUE TRIPTYCHS FROM THE CHURCH OF THE CARITÀ IN VENICE	62
A MADONNA BY ANTONELLO DA MESSINA	79
A MADONNA AT VIENNA AND ANTONELLO'S S. CASSIANO ALTAR-PIECE	98
THE ENIGMA OF CARPACCIO'S "GLORY OF ST. URSULA"	124
A CARPACCIESQUE MADONNA IN BERLIN	137
GENERAL INDEX	149
INDEX OF PLACES	153

LIST OF ILLUSTRATIONS

<table>
<tr><td></td><td></td><td>TO FACE PAGE</td></tr>
<tr><td colspan="3">ANTONELLO DA MESSINA</td></tr>
<tr><td>The Annunciation.</td><td>Syracuse</td><td>104</td></tr>
<tr><td>The Annunciation (Detail).</td><td>Syracuse</td><td>82</td></tr>
<tr><td>The Madonna</td><td>R. H. Benson Collection, London</td><td>83</td></tr>
<tr><td>The Madonna</td><td>Vienna</td><td>98</td></tr>
<tr><td>The Pietà</td><td>Correr Museum, Venice</td><td>87</td></tr>
<tr><td>St. Sebastian</td><td>Dresden</td><td>106</td></tr>
<tr><td>St. Sebastian (Detail)</td><td>Dresden</td><td>84</td></tr>
<tr><td>The Virgin Annunciate</td><td>Munich</td><td>85</td></tr>
<tr><td>The Virgin Annunciate</td><td>Palermo</td><td>85</td></tr>
<tr><td colspan="3">ANTONIO DA SALIBA</td></tr>
<tr><td>The Madonna Enthroned</td><td>Spoleto</td><td>109</td></tr>
<tr><td colspan="3">BELLINI, GIOVANNI</td></tr>
<tr><td>Drawing for a Saint</td><td>Academy, Venice</td><td>51</td></tr>
<tr><td>The Madonna</td><td>Bergamo</td><td>50</td></tr>
<tr><td>The "Galliccioli Madonna"</td><td>Bergamo</td><td>96</td></tr>
<tr><td>The Madonna</td><td>Frizzoni Collection, Milan</td><td>53</td></tr>
<tr><td>St. Justine</td><td>Bagatti Valsecchi Collection, Milan</td><td>38</td></tr>
<tr><td>St. Justine (Detail)</td><td>Bagatti Valsecchi Collection, Milan</td><td>40</td></tr>
<tr><td colspan="3">STUDIO OF GIOVANNI BELLINI</td></tr>
<tr><td>The Annunciation</td><td>Academy, Vienna</td><td>68</td></tr>
<tr><td>The Madonna</td><td>Correr Museum, Venice</td><td>66</td></tr>
<tr><td>The Pietà</td><td>Brera, Milan</td><td>69</td></tr>
<tr><td>Three Saints</td><td>Academy, Venice</td><td>63</td></tr>
<tr><td>Two Saints</td><td>Academy, Venice</td><td>65</td></tr>
<tr><td colspan="3">CARPACCIO, BENEDETTO</td></tr>
<tr><td>The Madonna and Saints</td><td>Town Hall, Pirano (Istria)</td><td>139</td></tr>
<tr><td colspan="3">CARPACCIO, VICTOR</td></tr>
<tr><td>Drawings for Heads</td><td>British Museum, London</td><td>134</td></tr>
<tr><td>Glory of St. Ursula</td><td>Academy, Venice</td><td>125</td></tr>
<tr><td>The Madonna (Detail)</td><td>Stuttgart</td><td>129</td></tr>
</table>

LIST OF ILLUSTRATIONS

TO FACE PAGE

CARPACCIO, VICTOR
 The Madonna and Saints   *Capo d'Istria*   128
 The Nativity and Donors
   Lord Berwick, Attingham, Shropshire   131
 The Presentation of the Holy Child (Detail)
   Academy, Venice   137
 St. Stephen (Detail)   *Stuttgart*   129
 St. Tryphon Taming a Basilisk (Detail)
   S. Giorgio degli Schiavoni, Venice   129

FOLLOWER OF VICTOR CARPACCIO
 The Madonna   *Berlin*   137

CIMA DA CONEGLIANO
 St. Catherine   *Wallace Collection, London*   45

FOGOLINO, MARCELLO
 The Madonna and Saints   *The Hague*   113

JACOBELLO DA MESSINA
 The Madonna   *Bergamo*   91

LEONARDO DA VINCI
 The Baptist   *Louvre, Paris*   5
 Drawing for a Madonna   *Louvre, Paris*   28
 Leda   *Former de Ruble Collection, Paris*   30
 The "Benois Madonna"   *Hermitage, Petrograd*   8

MANTEGNA
 The Madonna   *Bergamo*   89
 St. Justine   *Brera, Milan*   45

MONTAGNA, BARTOLOMMEO
 The Madonna   *Belluno*   121
 The Madonna   *National Gallery, London*   97

VIVARINI, ALVISE
 The Madonna and Angels
   Church of the Redentore, Venice   44
 Head of a Young Man
   Collection of Baron Schickler, Paris   59

STUDY AND CRITICISM OF ITALIAN ART

LEONARDO

I

As a boy I felt a repulsion for Leonardo's "Last Supper." The faces were uncanny, their expressions forced, their agitation alarmed me. They were the faces of people whose existence made the world less pleasant and certainly less safe. It was quite enough, for at that time I was not aware that, apart from the faces, a painting had any interest. Yet the figures, too, seem to have affected me, for I remember feeling that they were too big and that there were too many of them in the room.

Forty years have gone by since those first reactions towards a famous masterpiece, and they have offered me opportunities enough for coming to terms with it. For hours and hours I have sat gazing at it, with concentrated attention, receptive, eager to let it hypnotize me if it could. For as many other hours I have studied it as a scholar and as a critic. I have tried to find in it all that the adepts thought that they had seen, all that the rhetoricians persuaded me that they had felt; and I dare say I, too, ended in speaking with tongues.

If I did, it was to help my unbelief, for neither subtlest argument nor whirling dervish enthusiasm quite converted me. "Yes, of course," I would say, "the rhythm of the composition is truly wonderful, the articulation of the groups masterly, the action of the hands most effective. The details, too, even to the tapestries on the wall, are exquisitely rendered. But what a pack of vehement, gesticulating, noisy foreigners they are, with faces far from pleasant; some positively criminal, some conspirators, and others having no business to be there. No! I will have none of them. They are not company for me."

But I never dared say it out loud.

My next meeting with Leonardo took place in the Louvre, but it was years later, and I was no longer the child reacting to a sensation as a bell to its knocker, but a youthful aspirant for artificial paradises, full of elaborately prepared anticipations, determined to feel and understand whatever had thrilled and transported others. I would not be left behind or shut out. So I gave myself long exposures before the works of the Florentine genius, and particularly before his supreme creation, as I was taught to regard it, the " Mona Lisa." Standing on the slippery floor of the Salon Carré, breathing its lifeless air, with the nasty smell of fresh paint in my nostrils, occasionally stealing a moment's rest on the high stool of an absent copyist, I would spend the hours of long summer days trying to match what I really was seeing and feeling with the famous passage of Walter Pater, that, like so many of my contemporaries, I had learned by heart.

I wonder even now how far I succeeded, for brought up almost exclusively on words, I easily yielded to incantations and talismanic phrases. They put me into states of body and mind not very different from those produced by hypnotic suggestion, and I should have stayed under the spell, if only I had been kept away from the object. But the presence of the object disturbed coma and prevented acquiescence. Its appeals grew and grew until finally it dared come into conflict with the powers of a shaman so potent even as Walter Pater. My eyes were unglamoured and I began to look. What an enchanted adept died in me when I ceased listening and reading and began to see and taste!

What I really saw in the figure of "Mona Lisa" was the estranging image of a woman beyond the reach of my sympathies or the ken of my interests, distastefully unlike the women I had hitherto known or dreamt of, a foreigner with a look I could not fathom, watchful, sly, secure, with a smile of anticipated satisfaction and a pervading air of hostile superiority. And against this testimony of my instincts nothing could prevail. I argued with myself many scores of times that the landscape was mysterious and fascinating, that the conscious art of the painter was marvellous, for it was at once bold and large in conception and delicate and subtle in execution. Then the mass of the figure was imposing yet simple, the modelling persuasive, the existence convincing. I learned to revel in these qualities, to enjoy analysing them, and to dwell lovingly upon each point. I was soothed by the collectedness and fullness of her pose, delighted with the simple yet unobvious device by which her sloping shoulder is given a monumental breadth, and amused by the wary intricacies in the hair and folds. And besides, were not four centuries unanimous in repeating that "Mona Lisa" was one of the very greatest, if not absolutely the greatest achievement of artistic genius?

So I hoped that my doubts would die of inanition, and that my resentment, convinced of rebellious plebeianism, would burn itself out of sheer shame.

But neither happened, although in the meantime I too had become a prophet and joined my voice to the secular chorus of praise.

One evening of a summer day in the high Alps the first rumour reached me of " Mona Lisa's " disappearance from the Louvre. It was so incredible that I thought it could only be a practical joke perpetrated by the satellites of a shrill wit who had expressed a whimsical animosity toward a new frame into which the picture had recently been put. To my own amazement I nevertheless found myself saying softly: " If only it were true! " And when the news was confirmed, I heaved a sigh of relief. I could not help it. The disappearance of such a masterpiece gave me no feelings of regret, but on the contrary a sense of a long-desired emancipation. Then I realized that the efforts of many years to suppress my instinctive feelings about " Mona Lisa " had been vain. She had simply become an incubus, and I was glad to be rid of her.

But I did not dare even then. Who was I to lift up my feeble voice against the organ resonances of the centuries?

" Mona Lisa," however, was not the only masterpiece of the Tuscan Empedocles that I had come to the Louvre to worship. The high altar was hers, but next came the " Madonna with St. Anne," and here too I adored but failed to understand, until I understood and ceased to adore. Behind the post-hypnotic suggestions I was endeavouring to follow out, something in me rebelled against the arrangement and the expression. The Blessed Virgin, the Child, the landscape I joyously consented to, but St. Anne—she alarmed me with her airs of a great lady and look of indulgent omniscience. Besides, I was distressed in body and mind to see what she

LEONARDO

[Louvre, Paris.

THE BAPTIST

was doing. Seated on no visible or inferable support she in turn on her left knee alone sustained the restless weight of a daughter as heavy as herself. The silhouette, moreover, was unavoidably confused, and, but for the grace of incorruptible European sense, might easily have initiated patterns ending in the dizzy fantasies of South Indian sculpture.

The "St. John" occupied the altar opposite in the imaginary shrine to Leonardo erected by my masters. I no longer recall what spiritual rewards I was to expect if I inclined my heart and understanding to worship here too. But though I was too innocent to suspect the reason, I felt far from comfortable in the presence of this apparition looming tenebrously out of the murky darkness. The face leered at me with an exaggeration of all that had repelled me in the "Mona Lisa" and in the "St. Anne." And I could not conceive why this fleshy female should pretend to be the virile, sun-dried Baptist, half starved in the wilderness. And why did it smirk and point up and touch its breasts? Inspired by my good angel, I concluded that I was too young to fathom such mysteries, and so I gave this picture no further attention until I became a Morellian and decided that it could not be by Leonardo. Then for a score of years and more, something like a Freudian complex forbade my looking or thinking of the picture. At present I fear I must charge Leonardo with the crime. Possibly he did not paint it entirely with his own hand, for it must be conceded that no other of the few famous works of the master has so little beauty of line or colour or touch. But that only takes away extenuating circumstances that better quality would have furnished.

To follow out the post-hypnotic suggestion of my mesmerizers completely, I had to worship at two altars more, one dedicated to the "Virgin of the Rocks," and the other to the "Belle Ferronière." It took no too arduous spiritual combat to perform either act. I should have been glad if in the altar-piece the draperies, instead of attracting attention to themselves, served better to explain the Madonna's relation to the ground; I should have preferred a colouring less gray and dun, but I needed no enchantment to feel the humanity and mystery of the rest. The problem of the composition offended me not at all then, and indeed very little now, for it is not thrust upon one, and had Leonardo never sacrificed more to academic interests, it is likely I should have had no occasion to be making these confessions.

My whole heart went out to the portrait of the girl known as "La Belle Ferronière." I was on my own level again, in my own world, in the presence of this fascinating but yet simple countenance with its look of fresh wonder. Here too was colour that made me happy, supple modelling of quiet planes, and a contour as self-imposed as of a Laurana bust. For these reasons, however, the Morellian in me— only a secondary personality I venture to plead— began before long to doubt whether it could be Leonardo's. I assimilated it to Boltraffio because it was more like his imitations of its own self (as I perceived later) than to anybody else's type. I passed through a shameful moment when I resented this beautiful thing because I could not name its author. Happily I soon recovered my senses and returned to my early love. I fear, however, that in discussing Leonardo we cannot safely count her as his. But whose in all the world if not his, and if his, in no matter how limited a sense, in what moment of his career could he have created her?

So much for the objects of worship in the imaginary temple to Leonardo conjured up in my mind and firmly fixed there by the wise men whose incantations had enthralled me. At the same time, or soon after, I made acquaintance with three other works by the master for which somehow no niches had been prepared in my mental shrine. Two of them may have seemed relatively unimportant, namely, the "Annunciation" of the Louvre, and the "St. Jerome" of the Vatican. But the neglect of the third I cannot explain on artistic grounds, for ever since I made the acquaintance of this work, the Uffizi "Epiphany," I have had an increasing sense of its being, unfinished and blurred though it is, the most spontaneous, most comprehensive, and most satisfactory of all Leonardo's paintings. Its neglect must have been due to the fact that my inspiration had come from the stagnant pools of Academicism whose waters had not been troubled since the times that disregarded all that was not *contrapposto*, *chiaroscuro* and eloquence. It is true that these masters of mine, who, in their notions of the artists whom the intervening centuries always held in honour, remained victims of the dreary formulas of the class room, were the same who, when they got away from their horse-hair furniture and stippled prints, appreciated so poignantly a genius like Botticelli, although numerous generations begot of petty precept and mechanic prescription had never heard of him. Yet when it came to Leonardo, these victims of Academic teaching undervalued a masterpiece like the "Epiphany," because it was so little what they expected of that genius, being scattered and offering few opportunities for striking *contrapposto*, and concentrated *chiaroscuro*, and as few for grandiloquence.

I never felt called upon to take an attitude toward other paintings ascribed to Leonardo, for I did not accept them. There remains, however, the "Leda." Although the original is lost, copies tell us what she must have been like. She must have been twin to the blasphemous "St. John," as fleshy and as round, as contorted for purposes of *contrapposto*, and as murky with overwrought *chiaroscuro*. Given the ideal intention clearly manifested in proportions and expression, both she and her giant swan would have shocked me by their naturalism and over-display of abdominal rotundities.

But all these doubts, questionings, and spiritual combats might have remained confined to my breast —a breast once so subject to incantations and still filled with a *pietas* tending to make me loyal to the ancient gods. But one unhappy day I was called upon to see the "Benois Madonna," a picture that had turned up in Russia some few years ago, and has since been acquired by the Hermitage.

I found myself confronted by a young woman with a bald forehead and puffed cheek, a toothless smile, blear eyes, and furrowed throat. The uncanny, anile apparition plays with a child who looks like a hollow mask fixed on inflated body and limbs. The hands are wretched, the folds purposeless and fussy, the colour like whey. And yet I had to acknowledge that this painful affair was the work of Leonardo da Vinci.

It was hard, but the effort freed me, and the indignation I felt gave me the resolution to proclaim my freedom.

LEONARDO

[Hermitage, Petrograd.

THE "BENOIS MADONNA"

II

Of course there remains something to be said in defence, in extenuation and in explanation; and at the end there may appear a Leonardo quite different from the sorcerer held up by an uncritical admiration.

But first I feel called upon to meet the objection sure to be raised against one like myself, supposed to subordinate illustration to decoration, for being at the trouble to attack Leonardo's fame as an illustrator.

To begin with, and as a matter of fact, it has never been my intention to advocate the view that illustration and expression were of no consequence. In my "Florentine Painters," published more than twenty years ago, I laid as much stress upon "spiritual significance" as I did upon "movement" and "tactile values." But the last term was new, mysterious, and promising, and thus ended by attracting all the attention, the more so that I had taken the human interest and ethical appeal in works of art for granted, as calling for no definition or discussion, and had felt free to devote my zeal to the part of the theory whose strangeness demanded exposition and defence. Moreover, I insisted in that small volume and in others which followed, that a painting made up almost entirely of illustrative elements could never count as a great work of art, while, on the contrary, a great work of art might be as devoid of intentional illustration, as unconscious nature itself. This also could not but encourage the view that in my opinion the subject did not matter, and that its meaning was no concern of ours.

I venture therefore to say a few words about "Illustration." It will be remembered that I have comprised under that term more than used to be given to it, letting it stand for all value in a work of art beyond what is due to the immediate sensation of colour and the ideated sensations of tactile values, movement, and space composition. These values I have called "decoration," and in a sense it is true that spiritual significance is outside its purpose. We are, however, so centred, so socialized and so attuned that it is difficult if not impossible to avoid finding a meaning even where none was intended, and to cherish this meaning more perhaps than the object it sprang from. *Le sens n'est qu'un parasite qui pousse quand-même sur le trombone de la sonorité.* We may call this inevitable parasite "the over-meaning," for it is probably over and beyond what the artist himself had in mind, and certainly beyond what he could hope to convey with precision.

For the over-meaning is due to the fact that be what may the immediate instrument of the artist, his ultimate instrument is the human heart. And the heart is of a mechanism so subtle, so varied and so uncertain as to baffle any precise calculation of its working and to put it beyond the reach of accurate control. We know how inconstant, how capricious, how many-minded and irrational it is, and how when it does reason its reasoning is unknown to reason. (*Vide* universal literature *passim.*) It will respond easily and reliably only to the most primitive cries, those rising from the animal appetites and passions. Indeed, culture may be regarded as an effort to delay and to blunt these pre-human responses, and to use energy saved by preventing precipitation on that plane to lift us to a higher one. But once on that higher plane, the poor heart is left to itself, and it is so difficult to foretell how it will react that the amount of agreement we have come to with regard to matters beyond immediate animal need is sheerly miraculous. By what hidden ways, for instance, have people of a certain degree of civilization the world over come to identify given complexes of lines and shadows as the unfailing symbols of definite states of body and mind? Why should one look and bearing be recognized everywhere as intended to uplift us to the skies, and another as to degrade us to the gutter? But although we have arrived at a certain uniformity of reaction towards these appearances and thus to agree upon their meaning, it holds only for the extreme ends of the gamut of emotional resonance. Between flutter almost infinite shades of expression, the interpretation of which grows more and more doubtful as we approach the mean. Thus we all recognize the expression of horror and indignation on the face of an apostle in Leonardo's "Last Supper," and we see the lust of battle on the faces in the "Fight for the Standard," but how many of us not following out the post-hypnotic suggestion of the rhetoricians would agree upon what is behind Mona Lisa's look? Its over-meanings are not only as many as there are spectators, but more still, for it will appeal differently to the same spectator at different periods of his life and in different moods.

If the artist has no control of the over-meanings except of the most elementary kind, it would surely be wise of him to avoid those intricate and uncertain expressions which lay themselves out to manifold contradictory interpretations, and to confine himself to the simplest looks and attitudes. All others, far from setting up an immediate reaction of the kind to produce a sense of greater capacity and smoother working of our faculties, as the work of art should, are puzzling, bewildering, and even baffling, as problems proposed by science justly may be. For scientific activity, it should never be forgotten, finds its scope in the unravelling of puzzles, in the taming of what is bewildering, in the overcoming of what is baffling. Quite the opposite is artistic experience—it can for the spectator scarcely be called an activity—for it is intransitive and it aims neither at conquest nor capture, but at ecstasy. It comes to one not as a conscious reward of deliberate working toward an end, in the way that revelations come to thinkers and all other gifted men of science, but as an immediate, instantaneous and unearned act of grace, absolutely complete, and therefore, while it lasts, unchanging. For the artistic moment, as we may designate this ecstasy, is unaware of what preceded it, although it almost certainly was a long and severe training, and takes no thought of what will follow, although it probably will be a closer approach to perfection. But to consciousness the aesthetic moment is completely isolated, not to be modified and not to be qualified.

If that be so, it follows that, whatever merits "Mona Lisa" may have as pure decoration, although it is scarcely these that have perpetuated her fame, as illustration she is not really satisfactory. Looking at her leads to questioning, to perplexity, and even to doubt of one's intelligence, which does not interfere with our being fascinated by her, but does effectually prevent the mystic union between the work of art and ourselves, which is of the very essence of the aesthetic moment. That it is the fault of conflicting over-meanings I can scarcely doubt, for now we all know Chinese heads from Long-men, Hindoo heads from Borobodur, Khmer heads from Angkor, and heads from hundreds of other Buddhist sites, far more self-contained, far more inward, and far more subtle, which nevertheless, because of the untroubled clearness of the meaning, charm us into that ecstasy of union with the object contemplated which art should produce.

A portrait like "Mona Lisa"—a portrait of a person regarding whom we either do not have or do not desire to obtain other information—has, however, this advantage, that at least it cannot conflict with a character or event, or legend, or myth already fully formed in our minds. Educated people visualize, no matter how gropingly and vaguely, the heroes and the actions of story, and cherish a definite, if crude, expectation of how they are to be represented. The illustrator who does not come up to this expectation is thrown aside as unworthy, the one who opposes it is hated. Indeed, in my own generation, for all but a few, that was nearly the whole of art. I understand that this is no longer so, and art now consists of criss-cross dabs of dirty colour. Νήπιοι ουκ ίσασιν.

A soul-less dauber may get so absorbed in the mere technique of a painting as to remain unconscious of its meaning. But for the rest of us there is no way of ignoring the human appeal of a picture. We may throw it out of our minds, but it comes back through our hearts; and defiantly as we may pretend that it does not matter, its claims are the first to demand satisfaction. The most pressing of these claims is that the meaning suggested to us by the representation before us shall not contradict or oppose the spirit of the ostensible subject as conceived by ourselves. I naturally speak of those few among us who have autonomous artistic selves; for art, being for most people the eminent domain of "prestige values," is the chosen paradise of humbug.

It is there where kings stalk naked because they are supposed to wear raiment visible to the good and true only. It is there, too, where everybody is a Polonius who sees whatever the effrontery of a Hamlet bids him. There is therefore no such school of sincerity as the *examen de conscience* of aesthetic experience, for no other self-questionings make such demand upon our truthfulness, our sense, our judgement.

Yet even in art there are limits to credulity and submissiveness. We may, with Ruskin, see all sorts of depths in the candid puerilities of a Carpaccio, and all sorts of portents in the discoloured brushwork of a Tintoretto. We may even submit to the passes made over us by Pater using the "Mona Lisa" as a sort of magician's wand; we put up with apathetic and youthful St. Sebastians: but we cannot but revolt when asked to find delight in a work of art manifestly at war with its ostensible subject, as is impudently the case with Leonardo's "St. John."

The figure of the Precursor is one of the most clearly outlined, most definitely characterized, and most inalterable in Christian history. There is no better subject for Unanimism. His mention evokes in all of us the same ascetic, haggard image of obsessed proselytism. To satisfy this expectation, Leonardo gives us, not something non-committal, as Piero della Francesca or Antonello da Messina might have given, with an existence of its own overpowering enough to vanquish and replace a disappointment, but a well-fleshed epicene creature, with an equivocal leer, pointing upward with an operatic twist as if to invite us to look up, not to Christ first appearing upon the world, but to Bacchus clattering along with all his rout. No qualities of decoration, even if far superior to those found here, could ask for justice after such a blasphemy.

The case of the "Last Supper" is not quite so unimaginable. A Southerner at home among the ample movements, eloquent gestures, and vehement speech of an Italian market-place might find nothing amiss in Leonardo's presentation. But to us Northerners the sounds and sights of a Neapolitan crowd are deafening and fatiguing, if not positively repellant. And matters are not much improved by placing the figures in a way to bring into full relief their heroic proportions, the sinister or even criminal faces of some of them, and the purposeless grandiloquence of others. It only adds to our alarm and distress. We Northerners expect a quieter, gentler, more subdued humanity of Our Lord and His Apostles on the occasion of their last supper; and, although we are ready to tolerate conventions of type, scale, and environment up to a point, these must not flatly contradict either our notion of probability or sense of seemliness. I am too repelled by the illustrative side of Leonardo's "Last Supper" to be able to do full justice to the design as decoration, although it is possible that, if as decoration it was great enough, I could partly overcome my repulsion. Probably it is not great enough, but of that I may have another word to say later on.

It is scarcely necessary to discuss the other pictures that I have inveighed against; but we may remark, in passing, that for us of to-day, despite the shambles, stenches, and malpractices to which apparently a certain school of anthropology, inspired by *la nostalgie de la boue*, would reduce primitive Hellenic civilization, Greek mythology, woven as it is into our earliest and sweetest impersonal concepts, remains the realm of ideal shapes and symbolical actions. Distasteful therefore is every literal rendering and naturalistic interpretation of a mythological subject, and Leonardo's "Leda" is at once too heroic in size and too post-nuptial in forms, while the swan is far too big and real. Correggio's rendering of the myth is there to prove with what idyllic playfulness it can be treated, and with what absence of uncomfortable suggestions.

III

Although the question has already been half answered in the course of the foregoing pages, it will perhaps be more satisfactory at this point to meet it squarely. The question is how to account for the admiration lavished upon these pictures that I have been depreciating. One could impatiently reply "that it was all an affair of mesmerism, hypnotism, and suggestion." No doubt, but why did not the adepts select other pictures and other masters for their mystifications: why Leonardo in general and these paintings in particular?

To give adequate answers to these questions will be difficult until some such book is written on Leonardo in the Nineteenth Century as Italian scholars have given us on Virgil and Ovid in the Middle Ages, for there was a parallel in the fate of their reputations. In the absense of such a treatise, I venture to outline my own makeshift explanation.

It will be remembered that, in Mediaeval Italy, the Roman poets were changed into wizards who defied the laws of nature almost as flagrantly as if they were thaumaturgic saints. The last century was too enlightened to turn anyone into a sorcerer and miracle worker, and, besides, the public concerned was not of the ignorant but of the cultured classes. Education, however, does not destroy the myth-making faculty; it causes it to transfer its activities to fields less obviously impossible. And the man of letters who would smile at the vulgar herd, with its worship of material signs and wonders, will, in his imperious need of adoring idols, insist on deifying genius and magnifying its works. Once the artist had touched the skies with his sublime forehead, his creations were beyond blame and beyond praise. They were not to be analysed, no attempt was to be made to understand them; they were not even to be appreciated. They were there to bow to, to cense, and to pray to, for ever. As I recall the writings on art and literature that inspired my youth, it was very like a sacred dance.

The apotheosis of the artist, with which class especially we are concerned, is fairly recent. There were no complete instances of it in antiquity, which reserved this honour for the founder, the promoter, and the ruler, and scarcely ever for what we now, with a quite modern concept, regard as the man of genius—never whole-heartedly at least. The myths of Prometheus and Daedelus are to the point, for they are sermons in story against the pride of the intellect. Homer may seem an exception, but as he was directly inspired by the Muse, he ranked, although so high, yet only as her favourite.

To account completely for the worship of genius that sprang up a hundred years ago would probably be equivalent to accounting for the whole Romantic Movement. Much was due, no doubt, to the longing felt, sooner or later, by most people for identifying themselves with somebody or something beyond their own ordinary selves and workaday lives. Some of it followed upon the more than epic, more than legendary careers of Napoleonic times. Some, possibly to disappointment in military heroes, and a revulsion from their activities. It had been demonstrated that the world was as potter's clay in the hands of genius. If this world ended by drying and crumbling before it could be shaped to the heart's desire, the greater the need for a still more plastic realm of being where failure was less likely, and, at all events, less patent. For the Restoration brought back a number of things, but never the Rococo beatitudes about the golden mean.

Many people thereupon found satisfaction for their need of enthusiasm and adoration in the plastic realm of religion, but others in the still more plastic realm of art, and the worship the first dedicated to the Saints, these bestowed upon the great Artists. And for the first time in history the artist, from the artisan, craftsman, mechanic that he had been hitherto, was transfigured into a demi-god. He was endowed with qualities which raised him above the miseries of want and care, above the tyranny of habit and above material ambition. Like all other gods he was unconditioned. He was free to take any shape, and even to alter his nature. He could with his fiat create and destroy. The world was only an emanation of his being. Whatsoever he did was necessarily perfect, and whatsoever his divine hand had touched had the sacredness of a relic. Kings had no higher and more pressing task than to entertain him.

But be what may the reasons for the worship of the artist that seized the Western World a hundred years ago, no artificer of the past lent himself so well to apotheosis as Leonardo. Attainments and achievements of such quality in so many different provinces of art and science had never before been united in one man; and this man happened to be quite conscious and well aware of his worth. He was thus the first artist of modern times to consider himself raised far above the mechanic station occupied by his fellows. And he seems to have behaved in a way calculated to make his contemporaries take him at his own valuation. He dressed with originality and distinction, bore himself impressively. Surrounded, so to speak, by censor-swinging acolytes, he acted the part of hierophant and modern Empedocles, and was not far from being a precursor of Paracelsus. The remembrance, tinged with mystery, of these claims to sovereign consideration added to unmistakable and manifold genius, made him, as it were, the arch-type of the artist as well as the first and worthiest object of the new cult.

This transfigured Leonardo naturally shared in all the attributes of deity. He was unconditioned; he obeyed no law; there was no necessary sequence to his conduct; all that he did was perfect; and everything he left behind him was a relic if not a fetish.

It followed that as an artist there was nothing he might not have done. If it was too unlike the average aspect of his works, it was a sign of his having been lifted high above the laws of habit and the drag of mental inertia. If the painting was hideous, the god was poking fun at nature, showing how he could surpass her in ugliness as well as in beauty. And indeed it would be hard to get to the end of the pictures that people not so long ago cherished and adored as Leonardo's. I have found among them not only paintings from every region of Italy, from Spain, from France, from the Netherlands and the

Rhinelands, but even from the Tyrol and Styria, and they have been of dates ranging from fifteen to seventeen hundred.

Yet, as might be expected, it was the work of his more immediate pupils and followers that attracted most worshippers, because their authenticity after all was more penetratingly convincing than that of a Madonna painted on copper in the style of a remote descendant of Rubens. With rare exceptions, Luini's hand-painted chromos with their cosmetic smiles, Giampedrino's nut-brown inanities, Oggiono's pinched, sweetish faces, Predis' schematic miniatures enlarged to the size of life, Boltraffio's compass-outlined countenances were adored as Leonardo's. How little artistic appreciation and judgement were engaged we may deduce from the fact that Walter Pater, the most delicate, the most subtle, and the most exquisite of all rhetoricians, was enraptured with the stupid *pasticcio* of a "Medusa," and reproduced, presumably as the quintessence of Leonardo, a Milanese drawing of dubious expression and mediocre quality, on the title page of his "Renaissance"—the only illustration occurring in his works.

Conceive an image of Leonardo composed out of all these elements, and you will be assisted to understand the nature of the worship offered him in the liturgy composed by the fathers and hymnologists of his church. But well as it may account for the origin of the liturgy, it fails to explain just why the few pictures described in the first section of this essay, the "Monna Lisa," the "St. Anne," the "Baptist," the "Last Supper" and the "Leda," occupy the chiefest altars.

The truth is that these idols had stood on the altars of the humble primitive structure, scarcely a church but rather a "meeting-house" where disciples united to discuss, to appreciate, to praise, if not to worship. Their Leonardo was not yet a god. He was only a great inventor who made two discoveries, *chiaroscuro* and *contrapposto*, destined to transform the arts of design. It was as illustrations and triumphs of the new science and the new method that the pictures in question were first admired and prized.

In other words, the original interest in Leonardo was almost purely Academic. Although, like every innovator, he had many precursors, he was the first to perfect and to teach, to systematize and to practise a new science. He furnished models and examples of notation by means of light and shade chiefly, and of action attained by twisting the human body around its own axis. Like most other innovations these were double-edged. They enlarged the possibilities of expression, and made it possible at last to depict a face as agitated as in life, or looking a part as if on the stage. Reserve was no longer imposed by the imperfection of the instrument, and every one was now able to give full utterance to his precious soul. Man has never yet been known to decline an invention that puts greater facility and more power into his hands, no matter what the consequences. Inventors even in our day, when they are common enough, get appreciation and rewards somewhat out of scale with those apportioned to less utilitarian talents. Primitive man probably regarded them as gods, and Mediaeval and even Renaissance man as wizards.

In the arts of design as practised for thousands of years, invention has almost always aimed at finding instruments or receipts for quality. The striving is not necessarily useless, for, assuming that this is a rational universe, everything that exists must have a cause, and this cause must have worked through means ideally intelligible. But thus far we not only have failed to discover a mechanism that can be relied on to produce artistic quality, but we can scarcely conceive of using anything so complicated, so elaborate and so subtle as such a mechanism would have to be.

Nearly all the contrivances invented hitherto have served merely to conquer material difficulties of representation, and thereby to mask the absence of quality. What Leonardo did was to enable poorly endowed artists to satisfy an eye which seldom sees beyond its utilitarian needs. There is a challenge to the intellect in line from which chiaroscuro is free. Quality quite apart, a fault in drawing will strike thousands where a fault in light and shade will offend scarcely one. The latter process has therefore every advantage, if the aim be to produce an illusion, and for the self-same reason it can be formulated and mechanized up to a point. On the other hand the practice of functional line admits of no aids for the blind, no crutches for the unsteady, no short cuts and no substitutes for talent and hard work. The ungifted and ambitious find an enemy only less invincible in the exquisite surface of true, clear colour mated to functional line, and they would soon be brought to acknowledge defeat if *chiaroscuro* did not help them to blur, smudge, veil and hide. If the Western world lost for centuries its sense of colour, and could in our day, when the worst was over, believe that the negative and timid Whistler or the positive and crude Cézanne were great colourists, it was due chiefly to the practice of *chiaroscuro*.

Contrapposto, the turning of the body on its own axis, Leonardo's other invention, was not quite so fatal as the first, because it was less concerned with specific quality than with general design and illustration. But besides leading to the most jejune and tasteless affectations all over Europe, lasting to within two or three generations from our own, it had the more immediate effect of killing Florentine Art. No Tuscan painter or sculptor born after Leonardo's death produced a single work with the faintest claim to general interest. Happily its bad effects are now over, while *chiaroscuro* is still destroying many who might be artists, and helping to fame many others, the sight of whose painting is a mis-education. But when it was new, *contrapposto* must have seemed a contrivance as simple as it was effective in the hands of the unfortunates who had no cultivable instincts regarding the posture of the human figure.

If Leonardo was admired through the centuries, it was not because he was a supreme artist, but, paradoxical as it may sound, because he introduced inventions which seemed to make the teaching and practice of art easier, and it followed that those of his works which best exemplified *chiaroscuro* and *contrapposto* were the most constantly referred to, and the most highly esteemed.

And it was these self-same late works which for centuries had been admired chiefly, if not solely, for professional and even pedagogic reasons, that the Romantic rhetoricians, when they deified Leonardo as the sovereign genius, took over without question as the sacred objects of their worship. So they found themselves in the position of having to furnish reasons of their own for treating as master-pieces works selected by a different and more prosaic order of ideas. They might have been put to it if they had undertaken proof and demonstration. Priest-like they composed instead a hypnotizing and mesmerizing ritual. It kept us enthralled for two or three generations, and even now I am more than half horrified at this attempt of mine to shake off the spell.

For the sake of historical completeness, I must refer to one interest that, attaining great popularity toward the end of the XVIIIth century, contributed to the Romantic interpretations of Leonardo's paintings in general, and of "Mona Lisa" in particular. That interest, however, had nothing specifically artistic about it, nor indeed was it much more than phrenology and kindred futilities of that and more recent times. It was the interest in physiognomy fostered and preached by Lavater, and encouraged for a while by Goethe. No doubt it was largely responsible for a great many of the more elaborate utterances about the enigmatic and impenetrable depth of the "Mona Lisa."

IV

In the attempt to give the illustrative elements their proper place and due value in the work of art, and in the effort to suggest that the traditional admiration lavished upon Leonardo's most famous masterpieces had a professional and Academic rather than a literary and poetic origin, I have made statements which could easily lead the reader to anticipate the explanation I now venture to offer as to why these works, despite the praise of the schools and the adulation of the sophists, are not, to humanists like ourselves, quite satisfactory. The explanation is simply this, that in the paintings which arouse my resentment the aesthetic moment has been sacrificed to other interests.

The aesthetic moment has already been defined in the course of this essay as that peculiar condition of ecstasy which art should aim to produce. Whatever interferes with this rapture, no matter how worthy in itself, is a nuisance, and whatever succeeds in preventing it, as effectively prevents the coming into existence of the perfect masterpiece. It follows that besides much else which does not concern us at present, all questions of ways and means, essential though they be to the craftsman, must be carefully hidden away from the spectator. Hence the adage as old as Greece and Rome that the art of arts is to leave no trace of how art has been achieved.

But what can be more opposed to this than an interest so exorbitant in technical processes that it draws most of the spectator's spontaneous attention to itself! It is indeed being given the stone of science when one has been promised the bread of beauty. I know it is what the artist himself is apt to study and to prize in the work of art. *He* is quite right, for it is his business to learn how to create, and triumphal displays of mastery are his best schools and academies; but what have *we* got to do with all this, we who are not artists nor going to be artists, but aesthetic mystics craving to identify ourselves with the object of our contemplation!

The aesthetic moment in the "Mona Lisa" has been sacrificed to effects of *chiaroscuro* more subtly worked out, more insistently logical than any perhaps that had yet been achieved. It is possible that a further sacrifice was made to produce the enigmatical, impenetrable expression. On the other hand, it is conceivable that this expression itself was only a by-product of a technical preoccupation. Leonardo may have been thinking only of a mask, features, projections, dimples, and ripples which happen to have a parasitic human value, although for him they were merely tasks he had set himself in *chiaroscuro*. I suspect that, whatever the theory of his compendious series of scholastic recipes known and worshipped as the "Treatise on Painting," in practice he got so absorbed in problems of *contrapposto* and *chiaroscuro* as to forget spiritual significance. It is at least difficult to credit him with any clear and specific illustrative purpose when we find the same head and bust with but slight variations of expression, figuring now as the Baptist, now as St. Anne, and again as Leda. Being human countenances posed in a certain way, they cannot help conveying a certain meaning, but there is no sufficient reason for assuming that they owed their existence to another impulse than did, for example, Monet's haystacks. Those are no more studies in *plein air* than these in light and shade and posture; and it is only because the face is so immeasurably more familiar to us than a stack of hay, that we find more variety in the first than in the last. It is my impression that, like Uccello, like Baldovinetti, like Verrocchio even, the absorption in the science of his craft ruined the artist. His was a greater gift, and the ruin is not so lamentably obvious as in the closest parallel among his immediate precursors, Baldovinetti; but there is scarcely less of a contrast between his spontaneous genius, as manifested in drawings, and the quality of most of his highly elaborated paintings than there is between the exquisite works full of grace and loveliness of the youthful Baldovinetti, and the tasteless dulness of the same artist turned scientist.

I need not attempt to describe or define the quality and characteristics of Leonardo's drawings. The universal delight in them is scarcely to be questioned, and they certainly do not sin by being too painstaking and over-laboured. If they have a fault, it is, in fact, that they are at times too free and easy, and tend to be a little slack and caligraphic. With rare exceptions, which include some of the heads for the "Last Supper," their author seems to have regarded drawing no less than writing as but a means of note-taking, and left both unspoiled. Both his sketches and his prose, however, have a style of such simplicity, and candour, and unpretentiousness that one cannot but suspect that in temperament Leonardo was as natural as he was gifted, and that, to start with, he was endowed with a singularly happy sense of what is direct, swift, graceful, unstudied, and unaffected. Perhaps if his genius could have developed in a community less lashed by the furies of intellectualism, Leonardo would have avoided and escaped his errors, and would not have ended as the worst of corrupters, and the foremost forerunner of the Tenebrists and other pretenders of the later Cinquecento.

Unfortunately his passion for science, for schematization, for doing things by an Academic rule carefully pigeon-holed in a huge columbarium of other precepts and maxims, and, above all, his fascinated absorption in *chiaroscuro* and *contrapposto*, made him, as even a brief comparison between some of his paintings and the sketches and studies that served for them will attest, lose not only the sense of adequate illustration, and human significance, but his native gift of persuasive, natural, unforced action and composition as well.

To begin with the earliest, it is doubtful whether we possess any jotting done with an eye to the Hermitage "Madonna," but in the Uffizi and the British Museum we have a number of pen sketches made in preparation for other Madonnas of the same time, and in the Louvre we have the large design for one nearly identical in intention, pose, and action.[1] While all are singularly free and swift, natural and graceful, the Louvre "Madonna" stands out from amongst them as something which could be scarcely less premeditated, less laboured, or more like a flash of mind miraculously fixed upon paper. Nothing European hand has done is more worthy of the dematerialized art of the Far East; while—to be concise and comprehensive—nothing an Italian ever did was more pettily Dutch than the Hermitage "Madonna." We find the same striving for the utmost definition, the same fussiness over light and shade and minute distracting detail as in those *magots*, as Louis Quatorze justly called them. We see how, with every painstaking thought and laboured touch, something vanished of the noble daring and fearless freedom which inspired such a sketch as the Louvre "Madonna," until at last there was left only the manifest intention of displaying science, skill, and dexterity.

The autograph studies for the "Last Supper" are either slight pen jottings not to the present purpose, or chalk drawings far more elaborated. They are not yet so worked up as to rival in tastelessness with one or two overdone children's heads at Oxford from Michelangelo's worst years, but they have lost enough in freshness and sparkle to have created doubts regarding the authenticity of some of them. The fundamental faults, however, of this most famous

[1] Reproduced, p. 79, G. Gronau's "Leonardo" (London, Duckworth). This inexpensive little book contains adequate illustrations of nearly all the other paintings and drawings mentioned here. The text can be recommended as informing, appreciative, and free of humbug and re-echoing nonsense.

LÉONARDO

[Louvre, Paris.

PEN DRAWING FOR A MADONNA

of European paintings lie far deeper. On the illustrative side they consist, as I said early in this essay, in what is, for us Northerners at least, a vice of interpretation; on the decorative side, for all the genius displayed in the articulation of the grouping and the perfect accord of the rhythm, there are unconquerable difficulties in the nature of the subject. For certain subjects are unfit for serious treatment in the figure arts, and this happens to be one of them. It can be dealt with only as pure illustration by candid souls like Fra Angelico and Sassetta, who do not draw attention to the insoluble problems of the design. Leonardo's intellectual pride, on the contrary, was attracted by them, and the result is a composition consisting entirely of figures ending at the waist line, of torsoes with heads and arms but no abdomen and no legs. And in sober truth I come nearest to enjoying them as great art when I visualize them as museum fragments skilfully put together from the wreck of some noble pediment. But then I must think away many of the heads and hands.

We possess no sketches for the head of the "Mona Lisa," but a number of profiles from various periods of Leonardo's career, some nearly contemporary with her. Perhaps the most admirable are the one at Windsor of a young woman wearing a coiffe on the back of her head, and the probable portrait of Isabella d'Este in the Louvre. Both are of a naturalness and limpid simplicity not surpassed even by that highest achievement of earlier Florentine portraiture, the Poldi Profile. We cannot but conclude that it took an effort as gigantic as it was unfortunate for the author of these spontaneous creations to turn into the constructor of the "Mona Lisa."

Enchanting drawings of a beautiful girl stooping naked among the tall reeds to pluck flowers, while she fondles a swan, have everything to recommend them, both as human value and pictorial theme. Besides being positively attractive, and singularly free from unpleasant suggestions, the flow of all the curves, the rhythm of the nude, the bird, and the foliage have a beauty no less than lyrical. Yet all this had to give place to a monumentally sculptural conception odiously unsuitable as an idea and carried through with all the unsparing insistence of a pitiless chiaroscuro. There is, even in Florentine art, no more repulsive instance of confusion between the kindred but distinct arts of sculpture and painting than this half-realistic, half-heroic female of gigantic size courted by a swan no less huge.

But the most convincing instance of Leonardo's surrender of his native genius to professional problems and academic ideals is offered by the two versions of the "Virgin with St. Anne," the black chalk cartoon in London, and the painting in Paris. The first has perfect naturalness of look and posture, and a simple impressiveness of design, with nothing far-fetched and dear-bought. There is something truly Greek about the gracious humanity of the ideals here embodied, and it is no less Greek as decoration. I can still subscribe to what I said about it more than fifteen years ago: "One can scarcely find draped figures contrived in a more plastic way without going back centuries to those female figures which once were clustered together on the gable of the Parthenon." There was, however, no room in this cartoon for the exhibition of skill in conquering difficulties of composition. It required scarcely any subtleties of *chiaroscuro*, still less of *contrapposto*, and is not even pyramidal. So Leonardo discarded it, and contrived with logic absolute the Louvre design —a pyramidal design which, had it been completed,

LEONARDO

[Former de Ruble Collection, Paris.

LEDA

would have enjoyed a superabundance of *chiaroscuro*. Even in its present unfinished state, it revels in every kind of affected and acrobatic *contrapposto*—as artificial and masterly and wonderful as the most admired of forensic Latin periods.

The contrast between the cartoon and the painting is the more damaging as the former is already completely thought out in conception, and almost fully elaborated in essential execution, and thus escapes the possible retort that the difference is due to the advantage all slight sketches have over fully finished works. For in a sketch we expect the essentials only of pose and action, and trust the expression will be supplied in the achieved design. It stimulates us to the life-enhancing exercise of our own faculties by inviting us, as it were, to associate ourselves with the artist in completing his task. How true were Leonardo's instincts, and how faulty his theories, may be inferred from the fact that in his drawings, where there was little call to surrender native gifts to intellectualistic ambition, there reigns the greatest spontaneity and freedom. Among his autograph sketches, one at all highly finished is rare, and one unpleasantly laboured does not exist.

V

Florentine art tended to be over-intellectual, and of that tendency Leonardo was the fullest exponent. For in him it not only grew so conscious and so explicit as to get formulated into a series of axioms, problems and doctrines, but no other artist grew so indifferent to everything but their illustration and solution. Even Michelangelo, who is wrongly made responsible for the worst ravages of the theory of *contrapposto*, was not such a ruthless adept of it. In the one instance where he was going to abandon himself to its fascination as completely as Leonardo did in his "St. John," disgust got the better of him, and, after altering the posture somewhat, he let others complete the "Christ" of the Minerva. Besides, it never would have occurred to him to accumulate conflicting effects. In painting, he regarded fresco as the only manly art, and fresco admits no subtleties of *sfumato*. (It is significant, by the way, that Leonardo is not known to have painted in fresco.) Nor do we find trace of *sfumato* effects in Michelangelo's one finished panel picture. Leonardo's ideal, nearly realized in his "Baptist," must, on the contrary, have been to convey by means of *chiaroscuro* the impression, not of a coloured picture, but of one of those highly polished, dark brown, counterpoised bronzes associated with the names of Baccio Bandinelli and Gian Bologna. For *contrapposto* and *chiaroscuro*, in so far as they belong to art in any other sense than do studio properties and lay figures, or, for that matter, canvas and brushes, can contribute to the same end only when attention is drawn to neither; for the first can be properly employed by the sculptor alone, and the second by the painter, seeing that the one tends to the heroically monumental and the other to the freely pictorial.

Now it is this tactlessness, this recklessness, this blinkered way of pursuing an idea or formula or doctrine to its logical bitter end, never realizing the conflict with another idea, never seeing the absurdities, if not ferocities, it ultimately leads to, that we object to in intellectualism. With intellectual art in itself we have no quarrel, for it is the supremest form of art, the one from which all the others draw their inspiration, and without which there would be none deserving the name. Indeed, it was only when at last after myriads of years of manual and visual effort made by nameless precursors, the Greek mind, more immediately preceded by feeble Egyptian and Babylonian attempts, applied itself consciously and deliberately to problems of proportion, posture, rhythm, and composition, that the impulse to represent and counterfeit and adorn ceased to be mere handicraft, and became a clarified system of design worthy to be called art. For only then was it able to transcend the haphazard of the actual and to present us with an ideal, yet convincingly possible, humanity and humanized world. But at its best moments—those moments so brief, yet of everlasting consequence—Greek art never gave way to intellectualism, that is to say, it never allowed itself to lose sight of the aesthetic end by a too great absorption in the scientific means. On the contrary, it not only carefully kept these out of sight, but unhesitatingly sacrificed them to that high tact and happy compromise without which art is no more to be attained than life is to be lived. Still less would Greek art before Pergamon have abandoned itself to the logic of any one principle, no matter how necessary and fruitful the principle itself might be when used as an ingredient. But logic has been the ruin of most of the more ambitious and more intellectual art movements of the last eight centuries, from Gothic architecture to Cubist painting. For all we know, logic may reign supreme in a mechanical universe, but it enjoys a far less general obedience in the world of men, a world chiefly of rival desires, ideals, and dreams rather than of law. In this world every one and everything brings his or its own logic, and any system carried far enough is certain to cross another, if not to end in a blind alley or absurdity. Life is impoverished, not enriched by the fanatical adherence to one desire, one ideal, one dream fostered and permitted to hypnotize and mesmerize us into action. Few of the worst horrors of history are due to other causes, and it alone is responsible for the most monstrous horror of all which is being enacted now.

What is true of life is as true of art, which, regarded comprehensively, is its guide. Its ultimate aim is ecstasy, and any diversion that prevents our reaching that state is bad. There is no theory, no principle, no method that cannot be misused in this way, not even the highest, and most essential. Leonardo, for his part, misused two instruments whose loss, as a matter of fact, art would scarcely feel. In his most famous works they lie about like builder's and carpenter's, painter's and upholsterer's tools in what should be an ideal house. Wherefore I no longer rank these works with the masterpieces of the world's art. And I must confess that it makes me sceptical about the man himself, for a man who could be so carried away by misplaced interests savours more of the crank than the genius. Perhaps Leonardo was only the greatest of cranks.

I have tried, not a little frightened at my own temerity, to expose and bring down nearly all the famous idols of Leonardo's art, the "Mona Lisa," the "Last Supper," etc. If my words meet with any response in the minds of my readers, we may agree to inquire what, in fact, remains of Leonardo as an artist.

But first a word as to my temerity. The step just taken was, it seems to me, bound to follow upon the effort of Morellianism. Morellianism, surgical, pitiless, iconoclastic even as it seemed, was yet inspired by the Romantic ideal of genius and founded on the axiom that the greatest artist from cradle to grave never derogated from his greatness, and on its converse that whatever the great artist did was necessarily faultless. It was in defence of this that we Morellians fought for authenticity with the uncompromising zeal of Legitimists. It was, indeed, a brave fight and worthy, although it fortified the snob collector's blind confidence in mere names, and led him to accumulate unpalatable but authentic daubs by Rembrandt and other prolific geniuses. But the very method of establishing authenticity by tests so delicate, so subtle, and so complicated has led us on, little by little, to conclusions the exact opposite of the axiom with which we started out. Strict connoisseurship has taken the further and more painful step of recognizing that there are poor things among the autographs of the great artists, and that not every Bellini or Botticelli, Raphael or Rubens, Velasquez or Van Dyck is a flawless masterpiece.

To return to Leonardo and the question of what we feel remains of him as an artist, that, too, has already been more than half told in the course of this essay.

We may be bold enough to divide him up into two artists, so to speak, the Quattrocento, and the Cinquecento Leonardo. Of the second I believe I already have said enough. At the worst his works will remain masterpieces of great importance in the history and dialectic of painting. That they are bound to retain their pedimental prominence at the apex of the world's aesthetic achievement I doubt. There will be no return of this sort either to him, or to his Bolognese descendants, or to any other of the dethroned idols of our European past. Many people assume that admiration is merely a matter of fashion, and that we get tired and crave for novelty.

No doubt novelty is a mighty goddess, not unlike Kali in some respects. But we are not now where we were a century ago. Then it was a choice between the few schools, the few epochs, known to our tiny West European civilization. Since then, beginning with the truly godlike creations of Greek art, the art of all the rest of the world has been thrown open to us. Even now we are only beginning to make acquaintance with it all, and it will take generations before we understand it. By the time that this has happened, it will tax the aesthetic energy of cultivated society as a whole to grasp the masterpieces alone. The individual when bored with one kind will never have to go to a lower for want of one equally great. His *sacra fames rerum novarum*, his greed for novelty, will be able to vent itself without ever coming to an end of the best, although of course one cannot guarantee that he, too, may not occasionally be attacked by *la nostalgie de la boue*, and rummage among refuse.

Why indeed should this cultivated society of the future return to the " Mona Lisa "? There is nothing in her expression that is not far more satisfactorily rendered in Buddhist art. There is nothing in the landscape that is not even more evocative and more magical in Ma Yuan, in Li-Long-Men, in Hsia Kwei and a score of other Chinese and Japanese painters. There is less reason still why it should return to the " Last Supper," or the " St. Anne," or the " Baptist."

There remains the Quattrocento Leonardo, the author of all the drawings of whatever period, and some paintings. As a draughtsman his touch has a singular lightness and grace; my aesthetic life would be the poorer without it. It has given me real joy, and has helped to feed the secret springs of my being. And yet Leonardo can scarcely be ranked with the mightiest draughtsmen. Indeed, the word "mighty," so suitable to a Rembrandt or Dürer, or Michelangelo, sounds almost as out of place in connection with Leonardo as, let us say, with Watteau, the exquisite and lovable.

The Quattrocento paintings are not altogether easy to sum up just at present. The Hermitage "Madonna" obliges me to reconsider the canon of Leonardo's works. The man who could do a thing as bad as that may have done others, but the present estimate must be based upon two works only, the "Adoration of the Magi" and the "Virgin of the Rocks," although the second is no longer an achievement of the unspoiled Quattrocento. For me Leonardo is most himself, because most like his drawings throughout his career, in the happily unfinished "Adoration." Had he completed it, he might have ruined it as he did the Hermitage "Madonna." I I can believe that his best instincts prevented this act, for study has led me to conclude that when an artist was perfectly happy in his task he seldom failed to achieve it. But this unfinished "Adoration" is truly a great masterpiece, and perhaps the Quattrocentro produced nothing greater. Does this work alone suffice, however, to place its creator, where he has been placed hitherto, above all his contemporaries and predecessors? Was he really so much more the artist than the painter of the "Primavera," of the "Birth of Venus," and a score of other great designs? I cannot see that he is. I can see no reason why, leaving all other considerations out of the question, and judging him by his artistic achievement alone, the Quattrocento Leonardo should be placed above Botticelli. Happy for him if he falls no lower.

May 1916.

ST. JUSTINE OF THE BAGATTI VALSECCHI COLLECTION AT MILAN

THE "St. Justine" of the Bagatti Valsecchi Collection at Milan [1] is one of the entirely beautiful achievements of the Quattrocento in Italy. No artist of even that century of genius was so great that his reputation has nothing to gain were this masterpiece proved to be his, and, conversely, the fame of any artist, no matter how great, would be diminished by the removal of this painting from the list of his works. To any but the greatest names such a diminution would be all but annihilating.

And yet, odious as this task is to me, who twenty years ago, laboured almost fanatically to revive and enhance the memory of Alvise Vivarini, conscience obliges me to state the conviction I have had for some time past that not he but Giovanni Bellini was the author of the "St. Justine." It will be my endeavour here to justify this conclusion.

The picture is little known, although no one could be more hospitable than its owners, and no house could be more accessible than theirs. Milan, however, is a town in which one always feels eager to

[1] My cordial thanks are due to the Barons Fausto and Giuseppe Bagatti Valsecchi for the photographs which they had taken, especially for this article. Nearly all the Bellinis mentioned will be found reproduced in Dr. G. Gronau's " Künstlerfamilie Bellini." It is an inexpensive monograph which should be in everybody's hands, for a better informed, more candid, and more appreciative study of an old master is scarcely known to me.

GIOVANNI BELLINI

[Bagatti-Valsecchi Collection, Milan.

ST. JUSTINE

get further East or North, or South. Even I, who make a business of Italian Art, seldom find the leisure of spirit for more than a visit to the Brera. The tourist, even the cultivated one, has less leisure still, and besides, how is he to know that the "St. Justine" would be worth his while? Baedeker, omniscient and omnipotent, does not mention her, although he tells you that for a tip of fifty centimes to the porter you will be shown over the palace where she is enshrined. The "Cicerone" (once Burckhardt's) does indeed speak of her, and very appreciatively, but few people except special German students carry that estimable work with them. It will be well, therefore, to begin with a description of the picture, and with all due apologies I venture to quote with very slight changes the one that I wrote twenty years ago:[1]

"She is almost life size and full length. She steps forward on a narrow platform, the whole of her figure relieved against the curling blue cloudlets of a rose-gray sky. Her body is still vibrating delicately with motion, as if she were going to take one more step forward, and in sympathy with this vibration, the palm-branch that she daintily holds out in her right hand, takes a curve of the subtlest grace. The exquisite beauty of her oval, the almost morbid refinement of her features, the slightly trembling limbs, are in vivid contrast with the massive structure of her torso and the majestic height of her figure—contrast but not contradiction, for the refinement and the power are here so harmonized that the one seems the essential index to the quality of the other. She wears a jewelled diadem with a string of pearls over her forehead, and pearls in her flaxen hair. A jewelled girdle confines her high waist; and her

[1] Berenson, "Lorenzo Lotto," 2nd edition, p. 78.

mantle, held together over her breast with a clasp of jewels and pearls, falls in natural folds over her broad shoulders, and, leaving her waist free while clinging to her knees, is held in place by the left hand, which at the same time supports a book on her hip. From this point it falls like a maniple over her figure, and from under the elbow it descends in an almost straight but beautifully swung line nearly perpendicularly to the skirts of the mantle, which lie in quiet folds on the right, diagonally balancing the arm with the palm-branch to the left. In no other figure by any Italian known to me has the drapery been so successfully studied to bring out the rhythm, vibration, and dignity of the figure, and its relation to the space containing it, as in this panel by Alvise."

In twenty years my admiration for this masterpiece has only increased, but much else has changed. Thus, the intervening of other interests, the cooling hand and dusty fingers of Time itself, as well as an extended horizon and deeper insight, enable one to look not only much more dispassionately, but also more sympathetically and more penetratingly into questions that with youthful absurdity one got hot over as if they were causes rather than problems. To roast my pig, I had at that time to burn down the whole house. And such a little pig—the infinitesimal matter of whether Giovanni Bellini or Alvise Vivarini was the dominant influence in the formation of Lorenzo Lotto!

Although I knew well enough, even then, that to be a good teacher one need not be a great artist one's self, and although in the book in which all this was discussed I took great care to assert repeatedly that Alvise was inferior to Bellini, yet I was in love with the former, held a brief for him, and was only

GIOVANNI BELLINI

[Bagatti-Valsecchi Collection, Milan.

ST. JUSTINE

DETAIL

too happy to give him every advantage. And none greater than the attribution to him of the "St. Justine!"

I defended it with fervour, but I did not invent it. I took it over from my revered master, Morelli. Then a long time passed without my seeing it again, at least with active and not merely passive eyes. But finally, a few years ago, I looked once more and saw that it was by Giovanni Bellini. Morelli's error was excusable, for in his day artistic personalities had outlines that seem very nebulous when compared with the definiteness we have been able to give them since, and much then seemed probable that we now know to be impossible. The same reasons, to which should be added the not unamiable if rather stupid virtue of piety, as well as youthful zeal for my thesis, account for my blindness. It is curious, however, that the many students of Italian art who were neither disciples of Morelli nor at all partners in my enthusiasm over Alvise should never have questioned this attribution.

It will not be out of place to insist for a moment on our relative ignorance of twenty years ago with regard to Giovanni Bellini, and particularly with regard to his earliest phases. Morelli believed that the "Madonna" then belonging to Dr. J. P. Richter and now to Mr. Theodore M. Davis of Newport, U.S.A., was by Alvise. And, confining ourselves to such works only as have brought to Bellini's account something fresh in type or in tendency, we none of us then knew the very early "Madonna," which has found a home in Mr. J. G. Johnson's collection, nor the one with the beautiful oval that was in the Crespi Palace at Milan, nor the soberly majestic, Mantegnesque one discovered among his own possessions by the late Prince Trivulzio, nor the sublime "Ecce Homo" recently acquired by the Louvre. We none of us recognized as by Giovanni Bellini the "Resurrection," which has since then entered the Berlin Gallery. So little did we know him, that my attribution of this masterpiece to an artist who then seemed a great possibility, namely Bartolommeo Veneto, found much favour and is still tenaciously retained.

And each of these works was not merely added like a fresh layer to our knowledge of the painter, but each, as we mastered it, lit up and coloured and transformed our previous notions, so that now we not only know more of Bellini than ever before, but we know him more organically, know him, as it were, anatomically and physiologically, and can tell much better what he could and what he could not do. And no one so grows upon acquaintance. Indeed, it may be questioned whether Europe ever had a completer artist. His career shows sixty years of constant growth and fruition. He took the torch from Donatello and handed it over to Titian.

Knowing an artist, as distinct from knowing about him, like, indeed, every knowing which is experience and not hearsay, consists of all but unconscious physiological processes, with their somewhat more conscious mental reflexes, rather than of cognitive states. Indeed, I think it probable that in all recognition what we first become aware of is the likeness of the physiological condition into which a given object puts us to one already familiar from previous experience. If the memory of the previous experience then evokes an image which coincides with the object before us, we enjoy the pleasure of feeling the identity.

Something of this sort happened to me some years ago, when, as I was saying, I returned to enjoy the "St. Justine." I was not interested in the question of who made her, for, as I have explained, none of us had ever doubted that she was by Alvise. And yet the moment I came into her presence, and before I was aware of having looked, my whole physique responded as it responds only to a Bellini. The sympathetic system reacted to the retinal impression in a manner not at all corresponding to the one produced by Alvise, but, most unexpectedly to that brought about by his far greater rival; and so instantaneously that not only had conscious judgment not intervened, but not even complete awareness. And lo! when I finally did look, sure enough, I was seeing a Bellini. Thereupon in a flash all that was characteristic of the soul and substance and spirit of this master revealed itself to me, and so plainly that I could no longer understand how any of us could have been so blind to what it was.

My reader, however, has not presumably made this *chemin de Damas*, and it must be my endeavour to get him to understand it, and, if possible, to convert him to the truth.

* * * * *

Let us, in the first place, get rid of the attribution to Alvise. We know him now as well as he is ever likely to be known, for the works that have turned up in the last twenty years, welcome as they are, differ but slightly from those with which we were acquainted previously. He does not remain any longer a fascinating possibility such as he and many others once seemed. It is feasible, though this is not the place for it, to follow his career from beginning to end. He has his downs, and sinks so low (as, for instance, in the Barletta and Verona "Madonnas" and in the Brera "Christ"), that bad health alone can account for it. His ups we see in the Venice Academy altar-piece of 1480, in the one of several years later in Berlin, and in the "Madonna" of 1490 at the Redentore, and in the remarkable series of Antonellesque heads of which I have reproduced the best then known to me in my second edition of "Lorenzo Lotto" (George Bell and Sons 1901). Yet, giving him every advantage, and the benefit of every doubt, the "St. Justine," for its intrinsic value as a work of art, is measurelessly beyond his highest certain or at all probable achievement.

Indeed, I cannot conceive that if this most gracious figure were appearing now for the first time, any one of us would think of ascribing her to Alvise. What has she in common, beyond what is common to the work of all contemporaries and townsmen, with the stark and staring, clumsy and morose images that, with rare exceptions, comprise his entire repertory? The finest exception is the Redentore "Madonna" painted about 1490. Far be it from me to decry this impressive and even appealing work of art. Yet apart from the attractiveness of the music-making winged babies, there is little there in the way of intrinsic beauty that could not have been achieved with a pair of compasses. Successful the composition is, but it is really childishly rudimentary. And what else is there in this woodenly frontal figure? Little indeed that is essential art, yet this, his highest though it be, is perhaps Alvise's answer to the challenge he may have read in Bellini's Frari Triptych.

The "St. Justine," on the other hand, not only has an oval much lovelier than Alvise's, but sways with a rhythm as exquisite as it is stately. Although still archaic in construction and proportion, she is fully realized in the round, and that without any

[Redentore, Venice.

ST. CATHERINE
WALLACE COLLECTION, LONDON

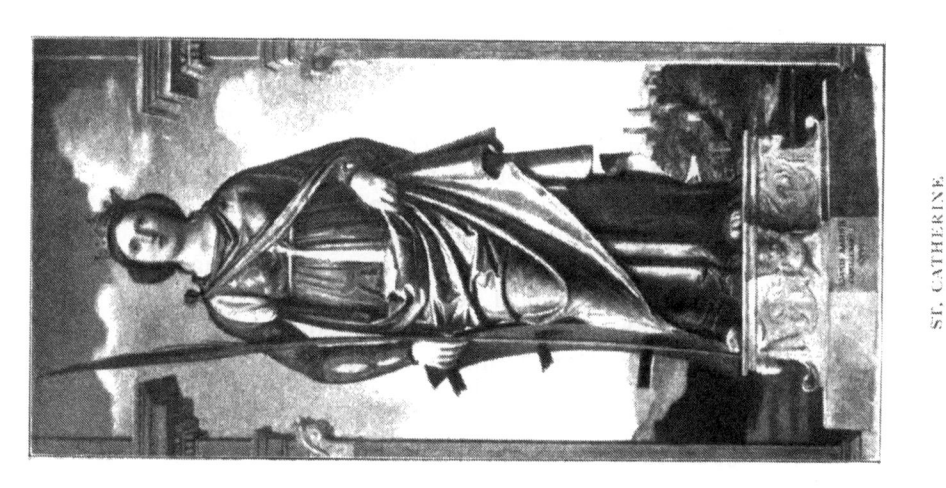

ST. JUSTINE
[Byer, Milan.

childish tricks of light and shade, and she is draped in a way that not merely builds up and reveals but enhances the figure.

Indeed, to such a degree is she beautiful, that she surpasses the model which must have inspired her creator, and this model was no other than Mantegna. You will find her in his Brera Polyptych painted in 1454, and there, too, she is a "St. Justine." Some of the differences between the two figures—as, for instance, the treatment of the draperies—may be considered to the advantage of the one or the other, according to the preference one has for the statuary's or the painter's art. But surely the Bagatti Valsecchi one has improved not only successfully but deliberately upon the pose, upon the proportions, upon the rhythm of the other, although that other is by Mantegna, and is a nobler, more harmonious, more spiritual conception than the one that inspired it.

And are we to believe that Alvise Vivarini, who in his highest achievements fails so signally of approaching Giovanni Bellini, here deliberately took up a masterpiece of Andrea Mantegna's to show how greatly it might be bettered?

Elsewhere he does not so much as betray any direct acquaintance with Mantegna. His earliest known work, the Monte Fiorentino Polyptych of 1475, is Squarcionesque in the worse rather than in the better sense, and, if revealing more Paduan elements than he could have absorbed unawares from his master, Bartolommeo Vivarini, it is not Mantegna whom he recalls, but rather Gregorio Schiavone.

But let us come down to details, and see whether, after all, our general impression can be mistaken, and Alvise remain the author of this great masterpiece.

The only head in his works which approaches that of the "St. Justine" is, as we already have noted, the one of the "Madonna" in the Redentore picture. But her oval is much rounder, the modelling heavier, the drawing harder. By comparison, her mouth is little more than a slit, her eyes are astare under the half-closed lids, and her nose is wooden— all as far as may be from the delicate pose, evanescent contours, and lovely features of the Milan picture.

The draperies of the "St. Justine" are, as I have already said, among the best understood in Italian art. See how they fall over her shoulder, how they cover chest and abdomen, how they encase the arm, how they reveal and communicate the inner substance of the figure. What do we find in the Redentore "Madonna"? Under her mantle there are no shoulders, and under her dress there is no chest. In the Venice Academy altar-piece of 1480, or the one in Berlin of some years later, the folds are indeed more functional, but they cover stocks and stones, so still and clumsy are the figures, instead of being, as here, instinct with the subtlest life. Even at their best, Alvise's folds never have the intrinsic beauty of line and rhythm that we find in this picture. In his earlier works, Alvise's draperies take folds as if cut with a knife in tin or leather, and although later they do get better, they are never like these.

One of the most delightful traits in this noble creation is the curve of the palm-branch held daintily in the right hand. It half evokes the idea of just the arch to frame in such a figure. Now Alvise found many occasions to put palms of martyrdom into his pictures. You find them in the Venice Academy altar-piece, in the Frari one, in the one in Berlin, and in nearly all his single figures of female Saints.

Never once has he made the least decorative use of them. They hold them in their fists or in their fingers, and that is the end of it.

Nor are the hands Alvise's. Only once does he display a hand which bears an accidental resemblance to one of the hands here. It is the left of a female Saint with a monstrance in the Vienna Academy, and I invite the reader to compare it with the corresponding one here, to see whether they show identity of origin. I grant, however, that the hands in themselves are the least successful part of the "St. Justine."

Finally, there is a sparkle, a freshness, a vividness in the colour and in the mere technique which are as different as possible (among contemporaries of the same school) from Alvise's. They have led the author of the picture, through his delight in the exercise of his skill, to seek every seemly occasion to embellish and to adorn—her hair with a diadem and pearls, her waist with a jewelled belt, her arm with armlet and again pearls. This delight in things that sparkle and shimmer extends even to the book, with its clasp, its studs, its gaufered edges and brocaded sides. And of all this there is in Alvise scarcely a sign. Few pictures of his are without a book, but never once do they approach the sumptuousness of this one; and his metal or jewelled surfaces, as, for example, the armour of his Georges and Michaels in his later altar-pieces, are dull and dead.

* * * *

The attribution to Giovanni Bellini might suggest itself from the mere excellence of the work, but it might also be reached by a process of exclusion. The only masters whose quality here entitles them to consideration are Gentile Bellini, Carpaccio, Montagna, and Cima. No one could entertain a serious claim on behalf of artists of the second rank, such as Bonsignori, Benedetto Diana, or Lazzaro Bastiani. All these names, big and little, call up, with one possible exception, artistic personalities which, for one reason or another, diverge widely from the spirit and style of the creator of this work. The one exception is Cima da Conegliano. In him there is something of the high refinement, the severe elegance of this figure. But, with all his gifts, he was neither sufficiently intellectual, nor, indeed, enough of a craftsman for it. Even he does not attain to this ultimate sense of inner substance. He produces somewhat the effect of porcelain, because, deep though he penetrates, he paints, so to speak, from without inward, while the "St. Justine" is painted from within outwards. Happily we possess a work by Cima which comes singularly close to our Saint, the "Catherine" of the Wallace Collection in London, and I reproduce her as a term of comparison. The differences should be as obvious as they are interesting. We see whence Cima drew his inspiration, but we see also that he could not have invented and executed this "St. Justine."

* * * *

Giovanni Bellini has been so hard to detect because, far more than any other great master, he constantly changed his types. In most artists you have one, two, perhaps three types of face and figure and character. These are soon learned, and the critic identifies them at once. After that, his business is merely to check his first impression by making sure that the forms and the draperies and the landscape are really his, etc., etc. For, say what you will, it is the type that puts one on the track.

Where, however, you have an artist as changeful, as innovating, as forward-striving as Giambellino, the facial type, the figure, the general character give at times no clue at all. And that is why such a very considerable share of his paintings have, until Cavalcaselle and Morelli, and, indeed, until the other day, gone under strange names. Only as I am writing this have I cast off my last doubts that the Vatican "Pietà" is from his own hand. It always seemed so Montagnesque. I remember, when the late Prince Trivulzio discovered among his possessions the gracious and tender "Madonna" that has since become so famous, we all said that, but for the signature, we might have taken a long time to see that it was by Bellini. An English critic of great distinction is convinced that Bellini's "St. Francis," despite its overwhelming spiritual virility, despite the austere beauty of the landscape, despite its matchless treatment of details, despite its confirming signature, is by Basaiti. Morelli himself, as I said at the beginning of this article, failed to identify the Davis "Madonna," and the "Resurrection," as stated earlier, enjoyed no credit as a Bellini until it entered the Berlin Museum. At one time I attributed it, on account of its landscape, to Bartolommeo Veneto. The fact is, that each of the pupils or followers of the great master tended to perpetuate through the career of a lifetime what had been only a mood or passing phase of their master's. Our acquaintance with these derivative talents resulted naturally in inclining us to attribute to them whatever bore close resemblance to them, until extended knowledge and greater familiarity led us back to the main stream.[1]

[1] I may add that I soon realized that the "Resurrection" could not be by Bartolommeo Veneto, and in the last edition of my "Venetian Painters" (1897) it is omitted from the list of his works.

All this was possible because, in the first place, the types were estranging. Then, it is true that at that time no one could know Giambellino's more intimate habits, those which escaped his own awareness and almost elude our scrutiny, as we can and should know them now.

* * * *

We need not take fright because, among Bellini's paintings now known, there is no other figure obviously and patently like the "St. Justine." In facial type, with just this dainty oval and this delicacy of features, there is no striking resemblance to anything else at all. Among extant works, the nearest likeness, and that is not very near, is to a "Madonna" in the Bergamo Gallery. There are resemblances also with the Angel on the left in the Mond "Pietà," with an Angel in another "Pietà" at Rimini, with the Child in the Brera "Madonna" with the Greek inscription, and with the St. Catherine on one of the pilasters of the Pesaro "Coronation." It is possible, moreover, that the burnt S. Giovanni e Paolo altarpiece might have furnished a close parallel.

The moment we get below the face we are better off. Putting aside questions of quality—for I have already insisted upon these more than enough—we shall find that the general structure and proportions, as well as the form and colour and technique, are sufficiently like Bellini's to confirm in every way our strong spontaneous sense of his authorship.

Structure and proportion are more or less common to all the artists living together in the same com-

---

At that time my impression was that it was a contemporary copy of a Bellini. I was hypercritical in those days, and besides the figures in the foreground are neither the happiest nor the best preserved in Bellini's works.

GIOVANNI BELLINI

[Bergamo.

MADONNA

GIOVANNI BELLINI

[Academy, Venice.

DRAWING FOR A SAINT

munity, and these, therefore, determine the school rather than the individual. In the "St. Justine," both structure and proportions are obviously Mantegnesque. Yet, within the Mantegnesque formula, no other Venetian figures come so near to this one as do Bellini's earlier ones, comprised between the "Transfiguration" in the Correr Museum at Venice, and the "Transfiguration" at Naples. Allowing for necessary differences, two figures could not be more alike than this "St. Justine" and such a typical one of Bellini's as the nude Christ in the London "Blood of the Redeemer." The same high waist, the same hips, the same very long legs. The likeness is nearly the same in all other figures so posed as fully to reveal their structure and proportions. An especially good instance is the Venice pen sketch of a male Saint with a book. This figure is, indeed, in every other way besides, so like our "St. Justine," and holds his book in such a manner, that I have the firm conviction that he must have been intended for a pendant to her.

Colour and technique cannot be conveyed either by photographs or by words, so I am reduced to begging the reader to believe that, if he could see the originals in connection with other works of Bellini's "Mantegnesque" period, he would agree that there could be no doubt that all were by the same hand.

And now for the minuter and more characterizing considerations, and first and foremost, because here the most important, the draperies. I will not insist again on their quality as function, nor on their beauty as line and rhythm, except to say that to the trained eye they are precisely of the kind that we find in all of Bellini's earlier works, and have, in common with them, an edge which tends to look brittle rather than smooth. This is most manifest in the lower part of the Justine's draperies, as it is throughout in the Frizzoni "Madonna," in the "Agony in the Garden," and in the Pesaro "Coronation," to take three conspicuous cases at random.

But let us leave general considerations aside, and examine how well the folds of the draperies here agree with Bellini's characteristic folds. In one of his earliest works, the Correr "Transfiguration," the folds on the Christ have not only the same general character throughout, but the drapery gathered up under His hand falls down almost exactly as it does in the "St. Justine." In the Correr "Crucifixion," an even earlier work, the folds cling close to the Virgin's right thigh and leg, exactly as they do here, but without, as yet, the same functional qualities. These, however, we find complete in the pen drawing for a Saint in the Venice Academy, which I have already mentioned as probably intended for a pendant to her. And in this figure the draperies fall from the knees and gather about the feet exactly as they do here, and with the same brittle edge. And we find this identical arrangement in Our Lady in the school version of a "Crucifixion" formerly in the Kann Collection. In the Naples "Transfiguration," besides the same general arrangement of the draperies, the Christ has the long fold sweeping across from under the left arm to the right ankle which we have in the "St. Justine," and again in the Venice drawing. The relatively horizontal folds under the waist in this drawing correspond to those in the Bagatti Valsecchi picture. Minuter likenesses still, escaping description, will be found with the folds in the Rimini "Pietà." The mathematically parallel small folds on the sleeve of the Saint will be found in the Child of the Verona "Madonna." Indeed, I must beg the

GIOVANNI BELLINI

Frizzoni Collection, Milan.

MADONNA

serious student, before dismissing my attribution of this great masterpiece to Bellini, to make a minute study of the folds in all of his works preceding and comprising the Naples and Pesaro pictures; for it is these folds, perhaps more than any other one element which confirm my conviction that it is by him.

Along with the folds, the hands are apt to furnish the best clue to the authorship of a painting, for the good reason that hands are usually drawn in a way which is habitual to the artist, and therefore characteristic of an individual rather than of a school. The right hand of the "St. Justine" happens to be an exception to this rule, for it is a close copy of the original by Mantegna which Giambellino had in mind. And yet a keen student who has taken the trouble to master the subject thoroughly, will find even in this hand the familiar outlines of Bellini and those folds in the loose flesh between thumb and forefinger which seldom are wanting in his earlier works. You find these same folds in the left hand, which is as typical a hand as he ever painted in those years. But for difference in position, it is the hand that you have in the Correr, Doge's Palace, and Rimini versions of the "Pietà," and in other pictures with slight changes in arrangement, as, for instance, in the left hand of Signor Frizzoni's "Madonna."

We have already noted, in comparing the "St. Justine" with Alvise's poverty stricken works, how sumptuously adorned she was, as if the creation of a man who rejoiced in his own labour, while his taste kept his exuberance in check. There surely is not a touch of adornment here which is not an embellishment—a quality of the greatest artists only. All these touches are applied in a way which again approaches this masterpiece closer to Giambellino than to anyone else. Under her throat her mantle is edged with an arabesque pattern made up, as it were, of compressed Arabic letters. This is a pattern taken over by Bellini from his father, Jacopo, as we see it, for instance, in the latter's signed "Madonna" at Venice. Giovanni used it often in his earlier years, in such well-known works as the Davis and Trivulzio "Madonnas," the Louvre "Ecce Homo" and the Berlin "Pietà." The diadem, the girdle, and the jewels are painted with that sparkle which never fails to appear in his genuine works, and which got more and more vivid until, as he aged, it became all but what it is in Giorgione and Titian when they treat metals or jewels—as if they were substances dashing back sunbeams in a foam composed of light instead of water. We are not there yet in this "St. Justine," but how much nearer than any other Venetian of that time could come! The pearls and jewels are painted as on the dress of the Trivulzio "Madonna," or on the cap of Doge Barbarigo in the Murano altar-piece. The heart-shaped stone serving as a clasp for her mantle under her throat is almost the same one which, as a brooch holding her kerchief together, we see in Dr. Frizzoni's "Madonna." Finally, the book, as we have already observed, partakes of the same sumptuous character. Indeed, it could scarcely be more splendid. Its edges are gaufered and studded like the volume in the Louvre "Ecce Homo," and the side is covered with a brocaded pattern of the quality of design affected by Bellini all his life, such as we see, for instance, in the Pesaro "Coronation," in the Murano altar-piece, in the London "Portrait of Doge Loredan," and in the S. Zaccaria altar-piece.

The clouds also, although treated in a way general to Venetian painting of the time, will yet, the more minutely they are studied, the more certainly be differentiated as peculiarly Giambellino's.

*   *   *   *

To this structure of observation and comparison, feeling, and reasoning, all tending, as I believe, to establish that the "St. Justine" is by Giovanni Bellini, it remains to fit the coping-stone. This is its place in its author's career, the approximate date of its execution. Without this, no attribution is perfectly satisfactory, and the more closely we can fit a work in with all the others by the master we would ascribe it to, the more certain may we be that we are right.

The exact chronology of Bellini's earlier years is as yet far from being so settled that we can be quite sure precisely which of several closely allied works came first, which second, etc. With regard to the "St. Justine," one thing is clear, that she belongs to Bellini's earlier years. As we have seen, all, or nearly all, the works we have had occasion to refer to in looking for points of likeness or identity to her, have belonged to that part of his career. No essential feature has called up any work later than the group dating from the end of this time, and comprising the Berlin and Rimini "Pietà," the Pesaro "Coronation," the Naples "Transfiguration," and several kindred works. If we try, however, to place her in the midst of this cluster, we become aware of distinct differences. Many of them are minute and subtle, and I dare not vex the reader's patience further by detailing them. Others are more manifest and no less significant. Thus, the proportions are slenderer and more archaic, and the whole pattern of the figure is consequently more Mantegnesque, as will be obvious if we compare the "St. Justine" with the Christ in

56   ST. JUSTINE OF THE BAGATTI

the Naples "Transfiguration." In the last-named and kindred works, one no longer finds the figures draped, as she is, painstakingly to display the curve between thigh and leg. The folds themselves have a smoother edge, and the outlines are less marked. In all these respects our Saint is nearer to the somewhat earlier group of pictures which clusters about the Frizzoni "Madonna." I should be inclined to assign her, therefore, a date close to 1475.[1]

*   *   *   *

St. Justine is one of the patron Saints of Padua, and are we to infer that ours was necessarily painted for that town? Not necessarily, although it is by no means improbable. But of one thing we may be certain, that she was not intended to be unaccompanied. She is far too large a figure (1.30 m. 55 cm.) for private devotion, nor is she the right shape for that purpose. In a church such a painting could only have formed part of a polyptych, and I come back to the suggestion I made earlier in this article, that the Venice pen drawing for a male Saint preserves for us Bellini's design for a companion panel to the "St. Justine." Indeed, emboldened by the number of masterpieces by the supreme artist which have been re-discovered in the last twenty years, I do not despair of seeing some day the painting prefigured by this sketch.

*   *   *   *

And what becomes of Alvise Vivarini, deprived of the glory of this splendid creation? Its loss almost annihilates him, as I have already said it must anni-

---

[1] Since this essay first appeared in print I have had occasion to study Bellini's chronology more minutely. The results will be found in my "Venetian Painting in America: the Fifteenth Century," chapters iii and iv.

hilate any man not of the highest rank. He is a strange problem, the solution of which may probably belong to pathology rather than to art criticism. What but despairingly bad health can account for such a drop as we perceive in the Barletta picture from the Venice altar-piece of 1480, a respectable if not inspired work? And there are other instances quite as bad, until, finally, after the later Berlin altar-piece, painted perhaps in 1497, he stops almost altogether, although lingering on in life until 1505. It is nearly certain that we possess no work executed entirely, or even in great part, by his own hand dating after 1500. The "Resurrection" at St. Giovanni in Bragora, the "St. Ambrose" altar-piece in the Frari, are largely the work of pupils.

Alvise would, therefore, almost utterly disappear from the rank of artists we do well to remember, if it were not for the series of remarkable heads, the earlier in the manner of Antonello, and the later more personal to himself, which I have described at length, reproducing many of them, in my "Lorenzo Lotto." Needless to say, that, when I got the conviction that the "St. Justine" was not by him, I began to doubt seriously whether this diminished Alvise could have painted these heads. I devoted much study to them, expecting to end by taking them away from him. I was not a little surprised, and greatly pleased to conclude that, so far as my science could inform me, they remained his.

These heads, too, are very unequal, and it is unfortunate that the only signed one, the Salting "Portrait of an Elderly Venetian," is one of the latest and least interesting. The Padua "Head of a Man," too, as well as the one from the Cohen Bequest in the National Gallery, are far inferior to such a fresh and dainty and pure presentation of a human being as we have in the "Portrait of a Venetian Lad" in the Salting Bequest to the National Gallery. And yet they all seem to hold together, as by the same hand.

Alvise, in the more Antonellesque of these heads, seems to have performed a feat not unlike Sebastiano del Piombo's. As the latter identified himself with Michelangelo to such a degree that he drew in a style that until very recently could not be distinguished from his model, so the former imitated Antonello with similar success. And perhaps the effort was as exhausting and sterilizing to the one as it certainly was to the other.

I seize this occasion to speak of a number of heads by Alvise with which I made acquaintance soon after the publication of the second edition of my "Lorenzo Lotto."

Four of these are from his later years, and thus less interesting to our present purpose, which is to confirm, if possible, the attribution to Alvise of the more deliberately Antonellesque heads. The most vigorous and interesting of them in design is a "Portrait of Colleoni," belonging to the Earl of Brownlow, at Ashridge Park. It has been published by Mr. Fry in the "Burlington Magazine" (XXI, opp. p. 48) as probably by Gentile Bellini. Perilous as it is to dissent from an authority so distinguished, I venture to think that whoever painted the Venice "Bust of St. Clare," and the "St. George" in the Berlin altar-piece (both undisputed works by Alvise) also painted this "Colleoni." Other evidence will occur to the student, and he must remember, in any event, that this portrait could not have been after the living model. The great condottiere died in 1475, the year of Antonello's arrival in Venice, and no Venetian could so quickly have assimilated the

ALVISE VIVARINI

[Collection of Baron Schickler, Paris.

HEAD OF A YOUNG MAN

latter's style, as completely as we find it here. Besides, Gentile is never so close to Antonello as is this head, and Alvise certainly was. He probably painted it about 1490.

The head next in importance was for some time in the hands of Sir George Donaldson, whence it started in search of a resting-place that it perhaps has not yet found.[1]

Another latish head, scarcely less ably individualized, and in a better state, belongs to Mr. J. G. Johnson of Philadelphia, and has been reproduced and discussed in my catalogue of his collection. A fourth portrait, painted evidently in Alvise's decline, is one of the less valuable of Baron Tucher's treasures in Vienna.

In the publication of the head that is at once the closest to Antonello and the most beautiful, Dr. Lionello Venturi has anticipated me. It is in the collection of Baron Schickler in Paris, and it is scarcely to be wondered at that a vision so clear, expressed in terms so simple, should always have been ascribed to the great Sicilian. But here again the well-informed student, such as Dr. Venturi has proved himself, needs no elaborate demonstration to perceive that it is by Alvise. Indeed, the pose is somewhat too emphatic for Antonello. The hair is drawn and lighted exactly as in the Salting "Head of a Lad." The mouth and the right nostril are more decidedly Alvise's, and thus easier to relate to his accepted works, particularly to the head of the "St. George" in the earlier Berlin altar-piece.

At the Old Masters' Exhibition of 1902 in London, there was to be seen the bust of a young man represented as "St. Sebastian," belonging to Mr. Romer

[1] The reproduction in "Gazette des Beaux Arts," June 1913, will tell its tale, to those who know Alvise, well enough.

60 ST. JUSTINE OF THE BAGATTI

Williams. It has since passed into the hands of Mr. Fairfax Murray. Again exhibited more recently, it was recognized and published as an Alvise by Dr. Tancred Borenius.[1] The design is closely Antonellesque, as all who recall the various "St. Sebastians" by Antonio de Saliba and his brother, Pietro, will recall. But, at the same time, the spirit of the whole, the nose, the mouth, are quite obviously Alvise's. It is, however, just as clearly by the hand, here already a little more itself, which painted Baron Schickler's portrait, so that, as the last mentioned confirmed the attribution of the Salting Head, it, in turn, is more convincingly Alvise's owing to this "St. Sebastian." The latter picture is, moreover, useful as a much needed connecting link between two such purely Antonellesque works as the Salting and Schickler ones, on the one hand, and the Bust in the Cohen Bequest to the National Gallery, on the other. We find that the hair in the first is treated very much as in the second, and that the chins also resemble each other. This Cohen "Portrait," by the way, I am inclined to date about 1488.

The head I shall now speak of is one with which my acquaintance is limited to the photograph kindly communicated to me by Dr. Gabriel de Térèy, the helpful as well as eminent Director of the Budapest Gallery, to which the original has recently been left by the late Count Palffy. It is a "Christ Bearing the Cross," inspired entirely by Antonello. Only, note that, unlike Antonio and Pietro da Saliba, or even Andrea Solario, Alvise does not copy the Sicilian. Here he is working as much as he can in his spirit, but with his own eyes. The modelling of the mask, its distribution as it were into masses, the

[1] Reproduced, as are also the Budapest and Frankfort heads, in "Gazette des Beaux Arts," June 1913.

drawing of the pupils, the nose and the mouth, as well as the treatment of the hair, all combine to leave only such doubt as to its being by Alvise as must remain in the mind of an honest critic when he knows a painting by means of a photograph only. It should be remarked that, if these precise curls do not occur in any autograph work of Alvise's hitherto accepted, we do find them in the head of the "St. George" in the Berlin polyptych from Alvise's studio (No. 1143), as well as in the Cathedral of Ceneda, in a picture by Jacopo de Valenza. Now it is a matter of common knowledge that Jacopo never invented nor even modified, but slavishly used Alvise's heads and motives and designs. Thus, in the altar-piece wherein the "Sebastian" occurs, Our Lady is an exact copy of Alvise's Barletta "Madonna" of 1483.

In the Stadelinstitut at Frankfort there is a brilliant and striking black chalk cartoon of the head of a young man with a great shock of hair, looking up to our left. No demonstration will be needed, I think, to show that it is by Alvise, drawn soon after the Schickler Bust.

Finally, there is just one more picture I wish to mention, because it is of some importance in Alvise's career. It is a "Madonna with the Baptist and St. Jerome," which I identified some years ago in the late M. Haro's collection in Paris. I see in the "Cicerone" for June 1912 (p. 419), that it is now in the Collection of Baron Herzog, of Budapest. It is a work Alvise probably painted at about the same time as his later altar-piece in Berlin.

April 1913.

THE FOUR BELLINESQUE TRIPTYCHS

FROM THE

CHURCH OF THE CARITÀ IN VENICE

WHEN I began my studies of Venetian art, more than five and twenty years ago, I felt strongly attracted to four figures of Saints, on gold ground, catalogued in the Venice Academy as by Alvise Vivarini. The tender solicitude for our conversion conveyed by the ascetic Baptist, the prelatical determination depicted in the concentrated figure of Anthony Abbot, the youthful candour of the good deacon Lawrence, and the skyey height of the dolorously patient Sebastian pierced with arrows, the severe simplicity of these figures as patterns, and their deep yet glowing colour, affected me powerfully. At that time they familiarized me with the name of Alvise Vivarini, and it is perhaps due to them that I began to take so great an interest in that painter.

It had, as yet, scarcely occurred to me to question attributions, unless they were flagrantly inconsistent with the little knowledge I had already acquired. Later, when I had learnt to test every attribution severely, I questioned this particular one feebly, because, by that time, the Bagatti-Valsecchi "St. Justine" had taken rank in my mind as the standard work of Alvise, and I found a certain correspondence, as indeed there is, between her and these

Academy, Venice.

Saints. I was not blind to difficulties, but I got rid of most of them by placing the Saints in some as yet unknown early phase of Alvise's career. For it should be remembered that at that time we supposed Alvise to have been born considerably earlier than the date now established. So much was still to be explored and mapped out! There was always the hope of coming across works that might serve as connecting links between these Saints and Alvise's earliest signed and dated work, the polyptych of Montefiorentino.

And there I left these panels, until a little while ago, when, after twenty years, I could again give undivided attention to the Venetians.

But meanwhile various things had happened. On the one hand, Prof. Paoletti had proved that these four figures were not, as I had supposed, isolated waifs and strays, but had formed, along with others which he succeeded in identifying, four triptychs painted before August 1471, for the Church of the Carità in Venice. On the other hand, we have, in the intervening years, become much better acquainted with Giovanni Bellini's earlier career, thanks to the many remarkable works that have been restored to him. We are thus, in fact, in a position to distinguish now, as never could be done before, between the Bellinesque and the Vivarinesque. (Indeed, until not so very long ago, thanks to the distracting splendour of Bellini's later works, and to our lack of acquaintance with his earlier ones, all that was at all archaic in Venetian Quattrocento painting was apt to be regarded as Vivarinesque.) Finally, as the personal equation in our studies, as in most others, is not to be suppressed, it is better science not to ignore it, but to take it into due consideration, in order to surmise what allowances to make for it. I venture, therefore, to be autobiographical here as elsewhere, because I believe that the critic's disposition is an important part of any problem, and not one to be overlooked. Part, then, of what had happened in the intervening years, in so far as I am concerned with the question of the four Saints and their companion pieces forming the subject of this article, is that, returning to them fresh, with so many years of acquired experience, I flatter myself that I can see more clearly and deeply than I did then, that I interpret and reconstruct better, and, perhaps more important still, that I have got rid of many prepossessions and prejudices. Now, I can only smile at the youthful whimsicality which led me to identify myself so closely with the cause of Alvise Vivarini that I could scarcely help disliking anyone who refused to take my estimate of him! As for Cavalcaselle, such was my feeling about him that it never occurred to me to consult him while I was getting up a subject. Only when my mind was made up, did I, if at all, look to see what he had said. Far more often than not, it did not occur to me to look at his, or indeed any other modern writings, excepting of course, always and everywhere, those of Morelli. Now, on the contrary, although I find Cavalcaselle's estimates and appreciations old-fashioned enough to be appealingly quaint, I am amazed at the correctness of so many of his attributions, and again and again I have been startled to discover that he had been before me in what I supposed were my own unanticipated conclusions. I am amused to see that some of my own old hobby-horses, Cariani for instance, had already been ridden by Cavalcaselle.

Returning, then, to these panels after the many intervening years, and looking at them in the light of all that I have seen, thought and learnt since, I

STUDIO OF GIOVANNI BELLINI

[Academy, Venice.

THE BAPTIST　　　　　　　ST. LAWRENCE

am surprised to find that they are neither by Alvise, as I used to think, nor even of his school, as Cavalcaselle thought, nor yet by Bartolommeo and Alvise Vivarini and Andrea da Murano, as Dr. Paoletti says in the last catalogue of the Venice Academy. I can now see nothing in them that is specifically Vivarinesque. What alone I do see are such close affinities with Giovanni Bellini in his earlier phase that I feel bound to conclude either that they were painted in his studio, or just outside it. It should, however, be borne in mind that the younger Bellini has more resemblance to the Vivarini than we are apt to realize when we think, as we are bound to do, of those marvellous achievements of his last forty years, in which he not only outstripped but entirely dissociated himself from his early companions and rivals.[1]

* * * * *

The four panels which first attracted my attention so many years ago, are now exhibited in the Venice Academy framed in the triptychs to which they originally belonged when in the Church of the Carità. The Baptist and Lawrence, along with an Anthony of Padua are numbered 621[b]; the Sebastian and Anthony Abbot, with another Baptist, have the number 621[a]. The two other triptychs, numbered respectively 621 and 621[c], contain, the first, a Nativity between St. Jerome and St. Louis, and the second a full length Madonna between St. Theodore and St. Francis.

[1] Many of Bellini's pictures referred to in the course of this article are reproduced in Dr. Georg Gronau's indispensable monograph on the Bellini. Unfortunately it is procurable in German only: "Die Künstlerfamilie Bellini." Also in Venturi's "Storia," vol. vii, part iv.

None of these is in good condition. The Madonna in the last is, according to Prof. Paoletti, a forged re-painting of a figure originally intended for a St. Ursula. The St. Theodore, also, is almost too much made over for reference, and so is the St. Louis. In all the gold backgrounds are new and horrible. And I may as well say at once that none of the panels since exhibited attain the quality of design or expression which belonged to the original four, except the one of the Baptist now framed with the Sebastian (621[a]). This Baptist is even finer than the one now framed with the Lawrence, and is, indeed, one of the few visualized conceptions of the Precursor worthy of a place beside Donatello's highest achievement, the Bargello marble.

On the other hand, the lunettes which originally crowned these triptychs are at least equal to the best of the panels. The very finest is a "Madonna" in the Correr Museum (Sala 11, No. 17) a fragment, according to Prof. Paoletti, of the lunette above the "Nativity" (621). The "Annunciation" in the Vienna Academy (No. 50) is all but as refined, and the "Pietà" in the Brera (No. 173) is quite as inspired. Only the "Trinity" in the Correr (Sala XV) is a trifle rougher in execution, although very large in design, and distinguished in feeling.

As the lunettes are, on the whole, of such excellent quality, we may as well begin our detailed examination with them, and first of all with the "Madonna" of the Correr Museum.

I cannot easily believe that a student, armed with our present knowledge of Venetian painting, who now looked at this "Madonna" for the first time, would think of placing her within any other circle of artists than Giovanni Bellini's. Indeed, I myself, who never before connected her with the group now

STUDIO OF GIOVANNI BELLINI

[Correr Museum, Venice.

MADONNA

under discussion, always supposed, as a matter of course, that she was "Bellinesque." The oval of her face and its whole cast is obviously his type, recalling closest of all, that curious studio piece, the "Madonna" in Berlin (No. 1177), where, also, the placing of the hands suggests resemblances. The Child's face, although almost grotesquely ugly, harks back to the one on the left in the Correr "Pietà," while His pose and action recall the Infant in the later Morelli "Madonna" at Bergamo. At the present moment, I am rather inclined to apologize for not including her in the canon of Bellini's autograph works. And yet, although the oval of her face is delicate and her look charming—in these respects superior to the Berlin "Madonna" already mentioned—she holds herself very badly, the draperies do not cover the body convincingly, the folds are summary, the Child's head is stupid, and the colouring unpleasantly red, so that I cannot believe that Bellini himself painted the picture. On the other hand, the action of the hands is highly Bellinesque and quite admirable. The drawing, however, as distinct from the action, is certainly not Giovanni's, particularly that of the right hand. Our safest conclusion, therefore, is that Giambellino invented the pattern of this picture in all its significant details, but that he left the execution to an assistant.

Who this assistant may have been, I cannot even guess. It is tempting, however, to connect him with the painter of the "Madonna" in Berlin before mentioned. That picture is a copy probably after a version, conceived perhaps some two or three years earlier, of the Bellini in the Verona Gallery, representing the Virgin with a Child standing on a parapet. In this Berlin copy the colour vividly recalls the Correr "Madonna," and I find in my notes that when I was last in Berlin I connected it with the *Carità* figures in the Venice Academy, although at the time I was unaware that the Correr panel belonged to them.

Be that as it may, whether the Berlin "Madonna" was or was not executed by the hand that did the *Carità* pictures, the fact that all of them can be so closely related to it, and the Correr one closest of all, amounts to a proof that the last-named, the Correr "Madonna," is not Vivarinesque, but as Bellinesque as the Berlin "Madonna" itself.

Taking this for granted —and the more readily as I recall reading somewhere in Dr. Gronau's writings that he too regards this "Madonna" as very Bellinesque—I shall now discuss the lunette in the Vienna Academy, which represents the "Annunciation" (No. 50). Its composition could scarcely be more rudimentary, consisting merely of a monumental figure in the middle, representing the Eternal, and two smaller figures balancing each other on either side, the Virgin kneeling at her faldstool, and Gabriel with the vase of lilies before him. Little skill and no dexterity are required for a pattern which nevertheless I find extraordinarily satisfying.

The Eternal has the mild benignity never to my knowledge given Him by the Vivarini, who make Him either more senile or more fierce, while here He anticipates Bellini's figure at Pesaro, or the one in his Vicenza "Baptism." The folds of His draperies have such whirls and loops as we encounter in Giambellino's "Agony in the Garden," in the Brera "Pietà," etc. The Virgin, in type and feeling, calls up another of Bellini's Madonnas at Verona, the one with the Child asleep on a parapet. The Angel is obviously next of kin to the one in the London

STUDIO OF GIOVANNI BELLINI

ANNUNCIATION AND THE ETERNAL.

[Academy, Venice.

STUDIO OF GIOVANNI BELLINI

PIETÀ

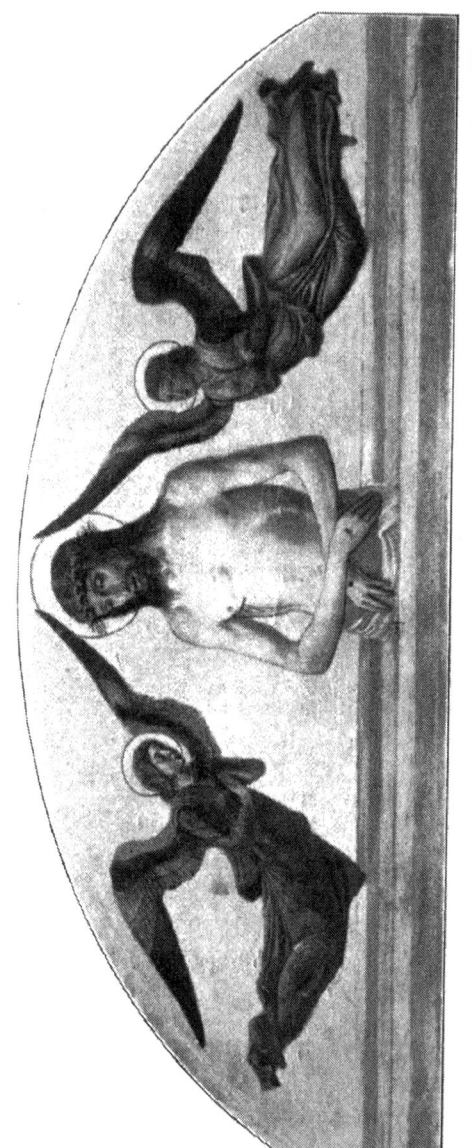

Brera, Milan.

"Blood of the Redeemer," and could scarcely have been conceived except by Giovanni himself or some one entirely under his influence. Here, too, I venture to conclude, the pattern is entirely Bellinesque. The execution was probably by the hand to which we owe the Correr "Madonna."

In the Brera we find a third lunette[1] of this series (No. 173). It represents Christ, crowned with thorns, rising out of His tomb, with His wrists crossed before Him, while two Angels, with wings deployed, hover at the sides in adoration. Here again I can discover nothing Vivarinesque. In none of their works do I find such depth of feeling expressed with so little emphasis. On the contrary, the head of this Christ is in every way worthy of the one in the London "Blood of the Redeemer," or of the Louvre "Ecce Homo," both of which it closely resembles in type, while recalling nothing in the Vivarini's work of the same date. The Angels, whose wings make a Moorish pattern framing in the Christ, are obviously of the same family as the one in the Vienna Annunciation. In this Brera lunette, then, I equally perceive the mind of Giovanni Bellini. As for the execution, the head of the Christ is all but worthy of Giovanni himself. It may be by the hand that did the first two lunettes.

The fourth lunette of the series is again in Venice, in the Correr Museum, and represents the Trinity between St. Dominic and St. Augustine. Here, too, there is a largeness of pattern and a freedom of handling, as well as a dignity of conception, that I am not familiar with in the Vivarini of this date. All, on the contrary, suggests Bellini. The head of the Eternal anticipates and resembles the type, more

[1] This and the Correr lunette are reproduced in the "Gazette des Beaux Arts" for September 1913.

youthful, it is true, of the Christ in the Naples "Transfiguration." The Christ on the Cross, both in proportions and in anatomy, resembles the one in the Correr early little "Crucifixion," and also the one in the Pesaro studio piece with the same subject. The Augustine and Dominic parallel, the male figures in the "Pietà" of the Doge's Palace, once dated 1472, and are a prophecy of those heroic prelates we find in the Pesaro "Coronation," or the Augustine of the Murano altar-piece. The hands of both the Saints are like those in the best of Bellini's known drawings, the one for a "Pietà" in the Venice Academy. We can thus safely discard here also their association with the Vivarini, and regard this work as a creation of Bellini's mind. The execution may be due to the hand that did the other three lunettes.

We can now devote our attention to the four figures which began by exercising a great fascination upon me, and ended by taking a place in my thoughts as typical works of Alvise Vivarini. My chief reason, though I was scarcely aware of it, for giving them such a place was their resemblance to the Bagatti-Valsecchi "St. Justine." The resemblance is certainly there, and were that picture the standard Alvise I then believed it to be, we should have to leave these figures as well to his circle. To me, however, few certitudes are at present completer than that the "St. Justine" is by Giovanni Bellini. As I have recently done all I could to demonstrate this thesis,[1] I will take it for granted here, and treat all resemblances to the "St. Justine" as to Bellini's

---

[1] Cf. the preceding essay. The Lawrence has a close resemblance to a Stephen on the frame of Bellini's great Pesaro "Coronation." There is a Baptist on the same frame which recalls and connects the two to be discussed presently.

credit. Such, for instance, are the long ovals of the faces of Lawrence and Sebastian, and the structure and proportions of the latter. In these respects, however, the Sebastian bears a much more obvious resemblance to the Christ in the "Blood of the Redeemer." Lawrence's mouth recalls the Virgin, and his hair the Child in the Correr "Madonna," and Sebastian's face has her ruddy tone. The Baptist and Anthony Abbot, like the Saints in the Correr lunette, have far more concentrated energy of feeling than any of the Vivarini at that time could have attempted to express without puckerings and contortions and grimaces. Alvise's "St. Johns," which used to seem to me to justify the attribution of this Baptist to him, are late works, painted some twenty years or more later, and were themselves probably inspired by Bellinesque creations like this one. The Anthony is worthy of Bellini's best, of his grandest prophetical or prelatical type, and I know nothing at all resembling him in any Vivarinesque work anywhere near this date.

The other "Baptist" in this series (now framed with the "Sebastian" and "Anthony Abbot") is, as I said toward the beginning of this article, so Donatellesque in feeling as to be worthy of a place beside the supreme Florentine's statue in the Bargello. Now Giovanni Bellini was notoriously subjugated by the genius of Donatello, while the Vivarini, on the contrary, were precluded from it by intellectual inferiority; for those only learn who can all but dispense with their teachers. The softest whisper will kindle genius, while all the thunders of Sinai, and all the choirs of Parnassus, will fail to rouse the dullard. The message comes to him through so many mufflings of misunderstanding that, finally, it is not so very unlike what he almost might have come to on his own account. That was the way the Vivarini received Donatello. Look at Alvise's "St. John,"[1] in the Montefiorentino polyptych, painted some three years later than the Bellinesque one we are now studying. Alvise's figure is angularly Squarcionesque in structure, and ludicrous in expressive action. Perhaps he had in mind the figure before us, and this is his aphasiac approach to it. Coming down to more specific points, I find our "Baptist's" nose recalls that of Bellini's Christ in the Correr "Transfiguration," and still more that of the Poldi Pezzoli "Dead Christ" (a studio picture). His right hand is very typical, and resembles the one in the figure just mentioned as well as in the Correr "Pietà," and even calls up such a late Bellinesque work as the Berlin "Pietà," now ascribed to the "Pseudo-Basaiti." The legs are drawn and modelled exactly as those of the Christ in the admirable school version of a "Crucifixion," at Pesaro.

In the triptych containing the "Nativity," the Jerome and the Louis are too much re-painted to offer material for study. The "Nativity" itself contains nothing, however, that I now recognize as Vivarinesque. On the contrary, the "Madonna's" oval, despite its heaviness, was probably designed by the hand which did the "St. Lawrence" in this series. Her kerchief and her hand both call up Dr. Frizzoni's "Madonna," by Bellini, and Joseph has the spidery fingers that we know in Mr. J. G. Johnson's "Madonna." The folds of the draperies are distinctly Bellinesque.

The remaining triptych, the one with the completely re-painted full-length "Madonna," and the other two panels as well, are so made over and in-

[1] Reproduced in my "Lotto," and in Dr. Borenius' edition of Cavalcaselle's "History of Painting in North Italy."

itially so uninspired as to be negligible. And yet here, too, the " St. Theodore," preserving the original action at least, recalls the military patron Saint in the *predella* of the Pesaro " Coronation."

* * * *

We may assume then, henceforth, that the four triptychs we have been studying are in essentials the creation of Bellini's brain. It would be interesting, naturally, to discover who executed them; if, indeed, it was one, and not, as well may be, a number of assistants. That, however, is a minor matter, the important thing being to establish that they are, in a sense, Bellini's.

Apart from the pleasure it gives a student to set things straight, and the value science puts upon having anything, no matter how humble, clearly ascertained, the restoration of these panels to Bellini's studio is not an altogether fruitless labour. It could not be that, in any event; for each great artist is, as it were, a star of a distinct colour and magnitude, in whose light we see each work we believe to be by him. A correctly attributed picture is a picture seen by the mind in its right light, best for it and best for us. A wrong attribution either obscures or illumines garishly. Associating these panels with Bellini, we shall look at them with different eyes.

But, even if our appreciation of them underwent no change, as ideally, in pure aesthetics, it should not, transferring them from the Vivarini helps us to a sharper outline of this group of artists, and approaching them to Bellini supplies us with materials which enable us to know and understand him better.

I will not dwell upon the fact that even a reputation like Bellini's cannot but profit by the addition of these lunettes and the best of the single figures. I will not insist on the interest it has for us to see how he treated certain subjects, like the "Annunciation," hitherto unknown among his works, or the "Nativity," thus far occurring only in the *predella* to his Pesaro altar-piece. The chief dry-as-dust interest these panels have, is what they can teach us regarding the chronology of Giovanni Bellini, for dates in his earlier years are deplorably scarce, and these four triptychs, as we know, were finished by August 2, 1471.

In the first place, they help us to win another date. The painfully disfigured, but still sublime " Pietà," in the Doge's Palace, is reported by Zanetti to have been dated 1472. To me, as to others, this seemed most improbable, and I was inclined to disregard it altogether. But the Correr lunette, with the " Trinity," in which the Saints bear such likeness to the ones in that "Pietà," incline me to disregard my former scepticism, and to accept the date as highly probable.

The truth is, that the chronology of Bellini's earlier years is still to be studied. Among the works that have come down to us, which we may safely call early, there must be such as were painted when he was very young, and others when he was well on the way to forty. Our instinctive tendency, when we think of the word *early*, is to emphasize its earliness as applied to anything. Consequently, we are apt to take "early" to mean *as early as possible*. This tendency we must resist, for we know that, in this case, the adjective adheres to works painted at any time before the artist's forty-sixth year, that is to say, during the most progressive years of any career. Mr. Johnson's, Mr. Davis', Prince Trivulzio's, and Dr. Frizzoni's "Madonnas," as well as the one formerly in the Crespi Collection, and the one recently discovered at Rieti, are all early Bellinis, but surely not all can be equally early. The Crespi picture, and even the Trivulzio one, are probably later than some others, and even Dr. Frizzoni's seems to me much nearer to the end than to the beginning of the early period.[1]

It follows that Bellini, although always a great artist, was far from a precocious one. In fact, he remained archaic until he was well passed into what is most people's middle life. Until then, his development seems curiously uneven, and in the broken light of our scant knowledge is singularly hard to follow. His father, Jacopo, his brother-in-law, Mantegna, the works of Donatello, may have provided too bounteous a feast and of difficult assimilation.

But suddenly, soon after 1470, when he was well over forty, he took a leap forward which in ten years or more carried him from archaic works like the four triptychs, which he conceived in 1471, and the "Pietà" of the Doge's Palace of 1472, to such resplendent works of the ripe Renaissance as the S. Giobbe altar-piece, the first that has come down to us of the great masterpieces to which the term "Venetian," used as a quality, really applies. Meanwhile, he not only created such works of genius as the Pesaro "Coronation," the Naples "Transfiguration," the Berlin "Resurrection," and the altar-piece at S. Giovanni e Paolo, besides a number of "Madonnas," but in these years he ceased being, like everybody else, the draughtsman who colours, and became the first *painter*, in the modern sense, that our world has seen. Perhaps tradition, after all, is right, and Antonello's presence in Venice in

---

[1] This question is discussed at length in my volume "Fifteenth Century Venetian Painting in America." The Rieti Madonna now belongs to Mr. Philip Lehman of New York.

1475-6 had something to do with expediting the change. I cannot, however, believe that it determined it in any essential or fundamental way.

In discussing the Correr "Madonna," we went so far as to suggest that its executant may have painted the Berlin "Madonna" (No. 1177), which we declared to be a studio version of a lost or unknown earlier variant of an original now at Verona. Even if the Berlin panel were, as I cannot possibly admit, an original, it would only strengthen the point I am coming to now, namely that the Verona "Madonna," closely connected as it is with the Correr one, must belong to about the same date. And this only confirms the conclusion some of us had already attained by other approaches. It is, however, a matter of considerable import, for the Verona "Madonna" is only one of a number characterized either by the classical draping (as in the Brera, Turin, Bergamo, and Rovigo versions, the Verona Madonna with the Child asleep, and the Venice Academy one with the Child blessing); or by the Virgin clasping the Infant with both her hands spread one above the other over His chest and abdomen; or yet again by her holding Him in her arms (as in the pictures at S. Maria dell'Orto and at Rovigo); or by various combinations of these characteristics.

Now as this group of "Madonnas" has always formed a bridge to connect Bellini's earlier with his later career, we cannot be too clear about when it was built. Its relation to our Correr "Madonna" of 1471 confirms independent conclusions that some of the earliest versions of this general type may go back to 1470. The advance within the group allows us to assume that some of them, like the Rovigo one, may have been designed as late as 1475. That

"Madonna" in turn points to the one in the Metropolitan Museum of New York, and to its companion in the Venice Academy, where, as Mr. Roger Fry pointed out, the Child is listening to the choir of cherubim. These last two "Madonnas," however, and what others go with them, must have been painted shortly after Bellini attained to the full maturity exemplified in the S. Giobbe altar-piece.

Before leaving the earlier group and bringing this article to a close, I would draw attention to the fact that one of them, the "Madonna" in the Brera, has folds over her lap and knees identical with the drapery of the Christ in the Pesaro "Coronation." For this and other reasons, both must be of the same date, and as the Brera "Madonna" is one of the later of the group, its date may well be 1475, and consequently that may be the date of the Pesaro "Coronation" as well.

Similar considerations, as, for instance, the close resemblance of the Child in the Brera "Madonna" to the Angel on our left in the Mond "Pietà," enable us to assign that work, too, to the same date. The Rimini "Pietà" is obviously somewhat later, and the Berlin "Dead Christ upheld by two Angels" must come between them. The Venice drawing for a "Pietà" must be a trifle earlier than any of these three. The treatment of the hair in this sketch is extraordinarily like that of the "Baptist" turning to our right among the panels which have formed the subject of this article, and the hands, as already noted, resemble those in the Correr Museum.

We have thus been able, with the aid of these four triptychs, to give more precision to the dating of a number of Bellini's early works, confirming what has already been arrived at by the few serious, leisurely students who have devoted their competent attention to the problem, notably Dr. Gronau, in his admirable monograph on the Bellini.[1]

May 1913.

[1] Since the above first appeared in print I found in the Metropolitan Museum of New York four figures on a shrine which belong to the same class as those on the Carità triptychs. They are published and reproduced in my "Fifteenth Century Venetian Painting in America." In looking over my notes I discover that in 1895 I saw at Münster a full-length "St. Barbara" of the same kind. She was numbered 39, but had disappeared before my next visit to Münster. I have not been able to trace her. It is a pity that the Prussian Art Collections do not publish a catalogue of all their nomadic pictures.

A MADONNA BY ANTONELLO DA MESSINA

It is a painful confession some of us have to make. Many a work of art fails to get our active and entire attention until we succeed in ascribing it to an artist already known. Once in a while we may be stirred by a nameless masterpiece of a manifestly high order; but we are so constituted, most of us at least, that we feel first baffled and then annoyed by an isolated fact. On the other hand, if we can bring to bear upon any given item a curiosity already well informed, and an admiration we do not fear to let loose, it gains greatly both in interest and value.

But for this trait of human nature, connoisseurship would at best be a form of sport less manly than many others and not so hygienic. It would perhaps take its rank as a game somewhat more strenuous than "Patience," and requiring less alertness than a geographical or picture puzzle. Connoisseurship pays its way by assimilating the isolated work of art to its kin, thereby giving it a clear title to the treasures of admiration and interest these have accumulated.

Instances readily occur. Let two suffice. The Dresden "Venus" must have been seen by hundreds of thousands of eyes, and yet no one looked at her. Then came Morelli and concluded that she was by Giorgione. Who has not admired her since? Only those who have not dared to say so, or, having said so, have not been heard! And likewise, at Bologna there was a Greek Head which must have been there for generations. No one noticed it until Furtwangler discerned therein a Pheidian type.

The insight of a Morelli, the power of divination given to a Furtwängler, are high gifts, but for their proper exercise they require adequate facts. And these facts are not always at hand. Data only too frequently are lacking.

Thus, Morelli in every probability was in the same room with the picture I am about to discuss, and his eyes must have lighted upon it. It is not likely that he lacked presence of memory, but there was nothing for him to remember. It is only since he died that documents have appeared which at last have removed Antonello da Messina from the realm of conjecture, and enabled us to give a completer and more defined image of his artistic personality.

I need not dwell upon the discoveries of various Sicilian scholars, who have found in the archives data for the life and work of Antonello, as well as for the life and career of a namesake of his, a nephew, whose works signed in the same way used to be ascribed to his uncle, to the utter defeat of every effort to construct a possible unity out of paintings, so different in quality, if not in pattern. Students are now well acquainted with these facts, and no one any longer argues that all Sicilian painting of the second half of the fifteenth century must be due to the great Antonello.[1]

[1] See an article by M. Henri Stein in the first semestre of 1909 of the "Gazette des Beaux Arts," under the title of "Antonello da Messina" (p. 35 *et seq.*). Anyone who wishes to enjoy an historical and aesthetical appreciation of an old master, should read Lionello Venturi's article on Antonello in Thieme-Becker's "Lexikon der Bildenden Kunstler." There, too, is a bibliography

Important as all this has been in clearing the ground, perhaps its most valuable result is that, owing to these documents, one considerable and remarkable work has been rediscovered, and brought down from its relatively inaccessible ancient dwelling at Palazzuolo Acreïde to the frequented Museum at Syracuse.

Had Morelli known this "Annunciation," he surely would long ago have anticipated us in the attribution I am now about to propose.

* * * * *

It is of a "Madonna and Child" in the well-known collection of Mr. Robert Benson of London, where it had been successfully hiding as a work by a chubby provincial named Marcello Fogolino. All of us who lazily assented to this attribution, were beguiled by memory into fancying a strong resemblance between the broad and empty countenances of the Venetic clodhopper and the homely but distinguished simplicity of the one before us.

Our Madonna is homely, but genial and even humorous—at least so she would seem to one acquainted with the restraint and sobriety of the serious Italian art of the fifteenth century. She is seen half length behind a parapet, and yet somehow she rises like a great pyramid out of the earth, towering against the sky over the severe horizon. She turns slightly to our left, day-dreaming with half-shut eyes, while she holds the Child. He clings to her with His right hand in her bosom and His left around her neck, as He looks at us, alert and

which was complete at date of publication, 1907. I take this opportunity of thanking Dr. Venturi for the photograph of the Syracuse "Annunciation" here reproduced, which he was the first to publish.

curious. He is half covered by the mantle that she wears over her sumptuously brocaded gown, which falls in noble folds from her head to her shoulders and over her back and arms down to her hips.

We are in the presence of a real work of art. The mass, or volume as the French call it, is as nearly geometrical as the legitimate demands of representation will permit. To have gone further toward the conical would have been to fall into affected simplicity, or into those interesting but scarcely pleasing deformations which the "Cubistes" of our own day are experimenting with. It is, however, only in works of a high order that an even tolerable harmony between the model and its geometrical mass is attained. We may judge how rare this particular success is from the fact that in European Painting the only conspicuous instances of it that leap into memory are the works of Giotto, Piero dei Franceschi, and Cézanne. The planes in works that achieve this success must be the simplest and broadest, as indeed they are in this figure.

The contours here are without any virtuosity or calligraphy, yet as subtle as they are bound to be when gladly submissive to their function of circumscribing the planes within the mass. Finally, the colour is lucid and warm, and of course neither hot nor gaudy.

If this appreciation is not exaggerated, and the "Madonna" before us is a real work of art, we must, now that we are ready to look for its author, expect to find him among the Great Masters. We shall not waste time disproving that it is by a Fogolino. I hope to persuade the reader that it is by Antonello da Messina. It is, at all events, not unworthy of him.

Not only is Mr. Benson's "Madonna" of a quality

ANTONELLO DA MESSINA

[*Syracuse.*

ANNUNCIATION
DETAIL

ANTONELLO DA MESSINA

[R. H. Benson Collection, London.

MADONNA

worthy of Antonello, but this quality happens to be peculiarly his own. In the first place we have seen that it displays a tendency to keep the geometrical figure most aptly containing the object to be represented. This tendency, as already pointed out by Signor Lionello Venturi, in his noteworthy article on our painter, is marked in all of Antonello's works where there is the slightest chance for its prevalence. Even his portraits, so convincingly individualized, display this tendency as far as subject permits. It is manifest in his completest masterpiece, the Dresden "St. Sebastian," and it is a pleasure to see how he has painted a purely geometrical form when he got the chance, as in the cylindrical column in his "Annunciation."[1]

For the present purpose the best terms of comparison are furnished by two other half-length figures seen behind parapets, namely, one "Virgin Annunciate" at Munich and another at Palermo. Unfortunately, as neither of these has a landscape background, they do not rise impressively like pyramids from the ground, as our Madonna does, yet they are so severely geometrical, and consequently so plastic, that they suggest busts by Laurana or the elder Gagini.[2] Both, moreover, are draped with the same search for the simplest lines and curves that will convey the fullest sense of the substance underneath them. The abstraction thus attained is at once liberative and creative, in each picture in slightly different ways. It is most obvious at Palermo, most complete at Munich, and most genial in our "Madonna."

[1] A curious display of this geometrical tendency in our Madonna may be noted in the conical fingers of her right hand.
[2] Both these sculptors may have influenced Antonello, and perhaps in turn have been influenced by him.

Such simple planes and enveloping contours as we find here, we discover everywhere in Antonello, but most of all in his heads. Almost all his portraits will manifest it, but perhaps the most suitable for us just here is the one in the Giovanelli Collection at Venice.

I understand well that all I have said thus far is open to the charge of being no more than somebody's impression. It is time now to attempt closer and more pedantic proof of my thesis.

* * * *

In the first place we shall look for resemblances of type and features. The strongest family likeness is with the Virgin in the Syracuse "Annunciation," and with a woman carrying a child, seen in the middle distance of the Dresden "St. Sebastian." Turn this last face from right to left, as ours is turned, and the resemblance is striking; nearly the same cranium and mask in each, while the cranium alone in our "Madonna" is even more like the one in the "Madonna" at Messina. The eyes here are slit upward a bit, as they are slightly in the just mentioned figure at Syracuse, and more markedly in the Munich "Virgin Annunciate." The nose in Antonello always follows the model closely, but the mouth more distantly. At least, so we judge, seeing how all but identical some of his mouths are in shape, drawing, and modelling. Thus, the upper lip, with its corners slightly turned up and stretching beyond the lower one, as we see it in Mr. Benson's picture, we find again in the "Virgin" at Syracuse, and conspicuously in the Johnson, Giovanelli, and Louvre portraits.

Coming now to considerations which are supposed to prove or disprove in a clenching way, but which

ANTONELLO DA MESSINA

Dresden.

ST. SEBASTIAN
DETAIL

Munich.] VIRGIN ANNUNCIATE

VIRGIN ANNUNCIATE [Palermo.

we shall do well to insist *dis*prove more convincingly than prove, coming to the treatment of the ears, the hands, the folds—in brief, to all the hiding-places where an artist's individuality may lurk undiscovered even by himself—we find what follows.

The only visible ear, that of the Child, tells nothing decisive, but not more against Antonello's authorship than for it.

Hands in Antonello's pictures in the position seen in our "Madonna" never occur again, and obviously resemblances are not to be looked for. I should, however, recognize the left hand here to be Antonello's by its shape as well as by its action. Perhaps it is the droop from the wrist and the foreshortening of the fingers which remind me of the Correr "Pietà." The thumb of this hand, firm and curving out, is more demonstrably our painter's. You can see that by looking at the Virgin in the Syracuse "Annunciation," or at the "Virgin Annunciate" at Munich, and you will find it, in an exaggerated way, in the Messina "Madonna." The fingers of the right hand we have already noted as conical, and thus in the line of Antonello's general tendency toward the geometrical. Observe that the high light on each nail is longitudinal, exactly as in the Munich picture.

The hair on the Madonna's head is plastered down over her forehead and parted in the middle, all with the utmost simplicity, as in every other female figure by Antonello known to us. The Child's hair is short and scanty, as it is almost always in the School of Messina.

The brocade of her gown resembles, as closely as is possible without identity, the brocades in the "St. Gregory," polyptych at Messina, in the Angel of the Syracuse "Annunciation," and in the Angel on our left in the Correr "Pietà." As for the folds of the draperies, how could both the very long-drawn ones and the shorter ones doubling upon themselves, as over our Madonna's left arm, be more like than they are to those we find in the Syracuse picture, in those at Munich and Palermo, and in the Antwerp "Crucifixion"? Even the striking peculiarity of the crease or two that we discover in her mantle, we find again over the forehead of the Palermo Virgin.

The landscape is neutral again.

* * * *

We may now venture to conclude that Mr. Benson's "Madonna" has stood well its examination, both from the point of view of quality, which we decided was in every way worthy of him, and from the point of view of more obvious, quasi-quantitative evidence, which also we found never worked against him, and nearly always for him.

Only one question remains to be settled. Does this "Madonna" fit in, and find its place in the chronological sequence of Antonello's work? Of that we now know too much to have any excuse for neglecting this form of proof. And we must maintain that it is perilous to ascribe any work to an artist without being able to say just where among his already accepted works it belongs. Mr. Benson's "Madonna" offers in this respect no difficulties whatever. Nevertheless, it is worth while threshing out the matter at length.

In type we found her to stand between the Virgin in the Syracuse "Annunciation," painted, as the documents declare, toward the end of 1474, and the women carrying a child in the middle distance of the Dresden "St. Sebastian." This masterpiece is not dated, and I am not acquainted with any con-

ANTONELLO DA MESSINA

Correr Museum, Venice.

PIETÀ

temporary documents regarding it. Yet it will not be rash to assume that it must have been conceived and carried through in Venice itself in 1476, or immediately afterwards, while the Venetian impressions of which it is so full were very vivid in the painter's mind. A further argument for this date is found in the figures in the middle distance, which, as has often been observed, recall figures in Ercole Roberti's Dresden "Predelle." No matter what that curious fact may point to in the relation between the two artists, no contact between them is at all likely to have taken place before Antonello's sojourn in Venice in 1475. But if I am right in my belief that Ercole imitated Antonello, and not *vice versa*, then Antonello must have painted his "Sebastian" while in Northern Italy, where alone Ercole could have seen it. Finally, to help place it, we have the further point that the soldiers here closely resemble those in the Antwerp "Crucifixion," dated 1475.

Other paintings which have constantly or occasionally furnished points of comparison with our "Madonna" are the Correr "Pietà," the Antwerp "Crucifixion," and the Palermo and Munich "Virgins Annunciate." Of these the "Crucifixion," as we have just seen, is dated 1475. The date of the others must be inquired into.

The Correr "Pietà," a ruin if ever there was one, and yet of such sublime design as scarcely to suffer from ruin, is so patently Bellinesque that we may safely assume that it, too, was painted in 1475 or so, most probably in Venice, which it seems never to have left.

As for the Palermo "Virgin Annunciate," in type, technique, and colour, in the trefles carved into her reading-stand, and most of all in the long-drawn folds of her draperies, she follows close upon the

Syracuse "Annunciation" of 1474. The Munich Virgin, on the other hand, is draped more soberly, with an elegance of simplicity, with a continuity of enveloping contours, with an economy of bulk, implying an artistic conception far advanced upon the Palermo figure, and much maturer. Technically, too, she strongly resembles a work certainly from the end of Antonello's too brief career, the Bergamo "St. Sebastian."

Mr. Benson's "Madonna," which in a sense may be considered as forming a trio with the two busts last discussed, is considerably more free and fluent than the Palermo one, but is yet in mass much more like it than to the one at Munich, which is more conical than pyramidal. For all these reasons we may date it soon after the Palermo "Virgin." This we already have put close to the Syracuse "Annunciation" of 1474, which again brings us back to 1475.

Antonello may, perhaps, have painted our "Madonna" after his first contact with Venice in 1475. His genius, still undeveloped, although he was forty-five years old, seems to have leapt thereupon to an immediate fullness of power and to an intense activity. Most of the masterpieces by which he has hitherto been known date from the *annus mirabilis* which followed. It is not likely that he would have become all that we know him to be had he never come North.

Since first publishing this essay, a consideration has occurred to me that may help to date Mr. Benson's "Madonna," and to throw further light on its author's career. It is this. This "Madonna" may possibly have been inspired by one of Mantegna's now at Bergamo. If this suggestion were well founded, it would follow, in all probability, that

MANTEGNA

MADONNA [Bergamo.

Antonello painted her while in Venice or Lombardy, and therefore not before 1475; and it would also follow that Antonello was acquainted with works of Mantegna, and perhaps with the master himself.

Certainly, Mr. Benson's and the Bergamo "Madonnas" have much in common, the patterns and the action in especial having many resemblances. Yet, as there is no identity, they might conceivably be the result of coincidence. Coincidences, however, are singularly rare, and I admit the possibility only because I have no time to look into the history in Venetian art of this precise motive of the Child embracing His Mother's neck and throat with both His hands. Yet, as it was used by Fra Angelico, it is not likely to have remained unknown. By itself, therefore, it would be indecisive, but it can scarcely be a coincidence that, at the same time, the Child is represented half naked, wrapped in a mantle.

For myself, I cannot avoid the conviction that Antonello had seen Mantegna's picture, and set himself the task of translating it into his own terms. At all costs, he must remain faithful to his more geometrical mass. In this instance it must be pyramidal, and consequently the Child must be more erect; and this necessitated the various alterations introduced by Antonello; as, for instance, His livelier look and more alert action. To furnish a solid base for the pyramid, we have the relatively horizontal arm of the Virgin almost parallel with the line of the parapet and the edge of the flat cushion.

Even if the resemblance between these two "Madonnas" need not necessarily imply that the painter of the one was acquainted with the work of the other, the likenesses in costume remain interesting and important. Both belong to the same phase of fashion, so to speak, and they must therefore have been designed within some years of each other. The exact date of the Mantegna is not known, yet it could scarcely be later than 1470 or so.

But for these resemblances, be their implications what they may, it might never have occurred to one to compare Antonello with Mantegna. The latter's genius was, of course, more varied and of wider compass; yet, looking at these two "Madonnas," I feel impressed, convinced, and sustained by Antonello's work far more than Mantegna's. There is a massiveness, a directness, a simplicity in the first that I do not discover in the second, for all its precision, thought, and science.

Like Bellini, with whom he had much in common, Antonello may have been fascinated by Mantegna. Traces of further indebtedness may be suspected in the Dresden " St. Sebastian," where the architecture as well as the figure sprawling in foreshortened perspective seem to recall the Paduan.

* * * *

Mr. Benson's " Madonna," is an important addition to Antonello's works. In the absence of considerable portraits of women and children from his hand, it fills their place, and from that point of view it is no exaggeration to put the Virgin's face alongside of Laurana's, and the Holy Child's with the best of Holbein's. Now that our attention is drawn to the picture, we find it a work almost as wonderful as that "Head of a Young Girl," by Vermeer van Delft, at The Hague, which, as an achievement, points backward to Piero dei Franceschi and forward to Cézanne.

* * * *

I have said all that I have to say in defence of my thesis that Mr. Benson's " Madonna " is a master-

JACOBELLA DA MESSINA

[Bergamo.

MADONNA

piece by Antonello da Messina. I must, however, try my reader's patience a little longer. The reason is this. In the Milanese *Rassegna d'Arte* for June 1912, there appeared an article by Dr. Tancred Borenius on a loan exhibition of Venetian paintings which had been held at the Burlington Fine Arts Club in London. In this article, Dr. Borenius refers to our picture, saying that it used to be ascribed to Fogolino, "but is now accepted as a work by Jacopo d'Antonello da Messina." Of proof, of argument, of discussion of any sort, not a word, unless we apply such terms to the continuation of his sentence, which runs as follows: "who [*i.e.*, Jacopo d'Antonello], thanks to the brilliant discovery of Dr. Toesca, has returned to us from the shades as the author of a signed work at Bergamo. Mr. Benson's picture is thus the second work that we have discovered by *filius non humani pictoris*. Doubtless, other works of his will turn up in time."

I sincerely hope that other works by Jacopo, or Jacobello, as he is generally called, will turn up in time. I confess, however, that it would not have occurred to me to ascribe Mr. Benson's picture to this modest artist, who knew his place so well that, eleven years after his father's death, his greatest vaunt was, as we see in the signature to his only known picture (the one at Bergamo), that he was the son of a more than human painter.

It behoves us to make the acquaintance of this, so far the only known picture by Jacobello. It has been staring us in the face for many years, but again successfully masked under an attribution which repelled and deviated attention. It is true there was a cartellino and something on it; but most of us have a shivering fear of these all but undecipherable inscriptions, and I, for my part, lazily took it for granted, for we were assured that the signature was "Jacopo Comolli," presumably a Bergamasque painter, whom I could very well leave over for that remote day when I should have time to waste on the obscurer artists of that region. Had I looked with eyes awake, I could not have failed long ago to discern how very Antonellesque and Sicilian the landscape and the folds were. The types, I must say even now that we have the Syracuse "Annunciation" and the "Virgins" of Munich and Palermo, do not somehow strike me as at all so obviously Antonellesque. They are far too sweetish. Of this, however, more anon.

Prof. Toesca, in the January number for 1911 of the *Rassegna d'Arte*, published a brief article, reading and interpreting the signature, and the date, which, by the way, is 1490, and pointing out all there was in the picture itself to confirm the signature. Then we all saw.

The reproduction of Jacobello's "Madonna" here offered saves elaborate description. The best way to get really acquainted with her is to compare her with Mr. Benson's "Madonna," and, incidentally, with other works by Antonello already recognized as his.

Let us first look at these two "Madonnas" from the point of view of volume and plane, contour, and draping. I realize that Dr. Borenius and other critics as eminent may have as good or better sense of all these qualities, and still be of the opposite opinion to mine. This, alas! is a sadder business than the question whether Nommisecca Fiesolano or Fannullone da Majano was the author of a crumbling fresco on the old road between their respective parishes. Yet will I venture to utter the conviction which is in me, and it is this. As volume, Jacobello's "Madonna" is neither pyramidal nor conical, nor anything else, for the reason that she has no existence at all, apart from what we are pleased to blow into her empty husk. The head, however, has somewhat more than the rest, and that, too, is universally characteristic of inferior painters. Of planes, it is enough to say that they have none of the largeness and breadth of the Benson " Madonna." The contours, therefore, are hard and niggling, although much better on the mask than elsewhere—again a characteristic of feeble artists. The draping is unfunctional, unconstructive, and altogether foolish. Not only is it of no avail in helping to realize the figure, but it has no value or beauty of its own. Compare it with the noble sweep and subtle line and fine rhythm of the draperies in the Benson " Madonna "!

And now let us grope as ants if we cannot trust ourselves in a broader outlook. Just observe the little bits of folds going their purposeless ways on the child's tunic, and the tissue-papery angular ones of the Virgin's mantle. Surely they bear no relation to those sober folds, as of heavy broadcloth, which are found in Mr. Benson's picture. The Child's hair, too, is very different, being curly and towzled. Nor have the hands anything in common, except the unfortunate fact—which, indeed, may have been the cause of the attribution—that the fingers of the left hand in the one picture have been imitated from those in the other. In the types and general design there is a school resemblance, of course, but the Bergamo Virgin is sweetish and pretty, while Mr. Benson's is homely and yet distinguished; and, as for the Child, in Jacobello He is simpering and sentimental, while in the other He is a vivacious, eager Infant. Consider, finally, what is implied by the different modelling of the masks of the two Children.

For me, it is hard to understand how these two "Madonnas" could possibly have been ascribed to the same artist, that I would fain believe this: that Dr. Borenius must have subconsciously felt that Mr. Benson's "Madonna" was by Antonello, but, being too shy to ascribe a picture hitherto attributed to Fogolino to so very great a master, compromised on giving it to his son, Jacobello.

I think the attribution quite indefensible; but, were it to be defended, it would have to be done on the assumption that it was an early work of Jacobello's. For one thing is beyond successful dispute, and that is the date of the Benson picture. Within the Antonellesque canon, this "Madonna" is a work of 1475 or 1476. Let them who can, prove that in spite of the date on it, the Bergamo picture was painted by Jacobello at that early time!

Among the works generally accepted as Antonello's, there is but one which might serve as a possible connecting link between the signed Jacobello and the Benson "Madonna." That work is the Palermo "Virgin Annunciate." In type she is nearer to Jacobello than any other of his father's faces— but yet how far!—and over her forehead her mantle has a crease, which crease is found again in Mr. Benson's panel and in Jacobello. But in him it occurs in a quite absurd position, over her left breast, like a ridge-pole supporting the rafters of a slanting roof. It might be argued that this was a worn-out mannerism of Jacobello's, betraying itself in all three works. Now it *may* turn out that the Palermo figure is a faithful contemporary copy of an Antonello by his son, Jacobello, for there is something not perfectly satisfactory in this picture; and, if that were true, which I do not believe at all probable, it would furnish a straw-to-a-drowning-man kind of support to the thesis propounded by Dr. Borenius. I believe he will find no stronger support.

January 1913.

※ ※ ※ ※

Revising this essay after three years and more spent in the study of Venetian Painting during the Fifteenth Century, I realize that, if it could be proved that the "Madonna" which forms the subject of this article had exerted a distinct influence on contemporary art, it would be easier to conclude that its author was a famous, and not an obscure man—the great Antonello, and not his mediocre son, Jacobello.

I can scarcely hope to offer proof of a kind that would convince everybody that such was the case. I can only declare that to me it seems highly probable. While studying Giovanni Bellini and Bartolommeo Montagna, I was led to perceive that the first was directly influenced by Antonello through personal contact, and the second indirectly, through the Sicilian's works. I believe that I can point to at least one "Madonna" by Bellini and to more than one by Montagna where acquaintance with either Mr. Benson's picture, or one essentially like it, may be reasonably assumed.

The Bellini panel was left a few years ago to the Bergamo Gallery, and is known as the "Galliccioli Madonna." Unfortunately it has lost its glazes, and it is difficult to decide whether it is an autograph or a studio picture. I am inclined to think that it is a studio version of a lost original, and that most of it was painted by the master himself, but scarcely the Child. I find a certain support for this view in the fact that another version of it existed in the collection of the Archduke Leopold Wilhelm at Brussels, and may be seen reproduced in a painting by Teniers still at Brussels representing a gallery in that collection.

Of all the Madonnas by Bellini known to me this is the most geometrical in tendency, and the most pyramidal in mass. The draperies are arranged with great study to produce the effect, and even in the ruined version before us it is easy to recognize a masterpiece and one of Bellini's finest achievements. In no other work of his do we perceive so plainly in the design how he was advanced and enriched by contact with Antonello. Of course it is hazardous to say that it was necessarily this exact Madonna of Mr. Benson's that Bellini had seen, but the more I study the economy of the folds the more does it seem probable that, if not this, then some very similar work, inspired him; and I seem to find confimation in the relatively realistic type of the Virgin's face.

A certain naturalism of aspect, an economy of draperies intended to produce a geometrical mass, and the employment of patterned brocades for Our Lady's dress lead me to believe that several Madonnas by Montagna as well were inspired by Mr. Benson's picture, or by a closely kindred work.

One of these Madonnas by Montagna, which happens to be as early as any extant work by him, was in the collection of the late Sir William Farrer, and was reproduced in the first volume of my "Study and Criticism of Italian Art." It is a picture designed at once under the personal influence of Bellini in his Antonellesque phase and of some work by Antonello himself, possibly the one now at Mr. Benson's. Another "Madonna," painted a year or two later, but still under the same influences, may be seen at Belluno (No. 35), and is reproduced in the " Bollet-

GIOVANNI BELLINI

[Bergamo.

"GALLICCIOLI MADONNA"

BARTOLOMMEO MONTAGNA

[*National Gallery, London.*

MADONNA

tino D'Arte" for 1910. But perhaps the most striking instance is the Madonna in the National Gallery with the Child seated on a book. In this design, as early as the Farrer one, the intention to attain geometrical mass is as plain as in any of Antonello's works. The only question is whether Montagna was in this instance thinking of the Benson picture, or had in mind some work, since lost, in which Antonello, in order to attain the pyramidal effect, had placed the Child so that He should break as little as compatible with naturalness through the silhouette, and interfere as little as possible with the geometrical mass.[1]

If it cannot be actually proved that Bellini and Montagna were acquainted with Mr. Benson's "Madonna," it results at all events from the discussion that they must have known a work singularly close to it. They certainly allowed themselves to be influenced by a design like the one of that picture, and, granted that that design is Antonellesque, as will scarcely be disputed, it is not probable that they would have so honoured a work by any but Antonello himself.

The dates we may assign to the Bellini and Montagna Madonnas are in accord with these results, for, as follows from conclusions reached independently, the Bellini must have been painted between 1476 and 1479, and the Montagnas soon after 1480.[2]

July 1916.

---

[1] When I began my studies it was the fashion to ascribe this Madonna to Fogolino, and I cannot help believing that it was this error which led to the absurdity of attributing the Benson Madonna to the same author.

[2] See my "Venetian Painting in America," chaps. iii and v.

A MADONNA AT VIENNA AND ANTO-NELLO'S S. CASSIANO ALTAR-PIECE

FOR five and twenty years a certain Madonna at Vienna interested and baffled me. When it first attracted my attention it was ascribed to Giovanni Bellini, but I gave this attribution no thought, for the painting obviously was not by Bellini. To me at that time it suggested rather a master like Boccaccio Boccaccino, whose facial oval, large round eyes, and rich tone it recalled. Yet I was not really content to ascribe it to him, and ten years ago, as a counsel of despair, I included it in my " North Italian Painters" as a work that might conceivably have been done by the more shadowy " Pseudo-Boccaccino."

I do not feel ashamed of having approached the Vienna Madonna to Boccaccino's manner, because the resemblances are there, and, in the state of knowledge then prevailing, no other painter was so well entitled to claim it. I feel even less ashamed of having included it with a question mark in the list of the Pseudo-Boccaccino's works because that master, after he had been differentiated from Boccaccino, had even more claims upon it. They were, however, not sufficient. Perhaps if I had been austerely scientific I should have omitted any mention of the picture; but it has, however, been my practice to include interesting and important works, the further study of which could not but be fruitful, under the painters with whose styles they had most in common. The question mark was there as a

ANTONELLO DA MESSINA

[Vienna.

MADONNA

warning that the inclusion was to be regarded as a direction of research rather than as a settled attribution. An unknown picture thus became a subject of discourse, and more than one has thereby ended with finding its real author.

Meanwhile, and during years which, owing to other occupations, I could not dedicate to the systematic pursuit of Venetian Art, new documents and new works had appeared which clarified, enlarged and intensified our acquaintance with Antonello da Messina. A number of fixed dates were acquired without which it had been disputable just what decades of the fifteenth century were traversed by his career, making it, consequently, almost impossible to know what exactly might be expected of him. But now we can be quite sure of certain points, as, for instance, that a picture dated after 1479, the year of the great Antonello's death, cannot be his. In recent times also, his most informing work, the large "Annunciation" from Palazzolo Acreide, was discovered; busts like the "Virgins Annunciate" of Palermo and Munich first appeared; and that exquisite masterpiece, the National Gallery "St. Jerome," was accepted by everybody as his. Almost as soon as I found the leisure to assimilate this new knowledge, I realized that the Vienna "Madonna" which had seemed close to Boccaccio, and closer still to the Pseudo-Boccaccino, was closest of all to Antonello.[1]

At about the same time my American neighbour in Florence, Mr. Henry Cannon, acquired a small copy of this Madonna, painted by Teniers, no doubt for the purpose of being engraved in his "Theatrum

[1] Meanwhile Dr. Borenius published in the "Burlington Magazine" for May 1913 his own independent conclusions regarding the Vienna picture, pointing out its relation to Antonello.

Pictoricum," the sumptuous volume containing reproductions of the most esteemed masterpieces in the collection of the Archduke Leopold Wilhelm. I looked into the volume and sure enough our Madonna was there reproduced as a work of Giovanni Bellini's. But as in the seventeenth century the attribution of a picture to that genius meant no more than that it was a fifteenth century Venetian picture of price, I felt assured that the Vienna "Madonna" had come from Venice, where tradition had handed down a sense of its interest and value. Another important fact regarding it resulted from a close study of Teniers' copy, namely that after this was made the original had been slightly cut down. Somehow this suggested to me the probability that the Vienna panel was only a fragment, and the possibility that it was a fragment of Antonello's epoch-making S. Cassiano altar-piece.

On my next visit to Vienna I communicated my idea to Count Lanckoronski, to Dr. Gluck and to Professor Dvořak, and succeeded in engaging their interest, and procuring the promise that the picture should be cleaned. For, as it was considerably repainted, I hoped that cleaning would uncover definite proofs that it was but a fragment. Some time passed, the war intervened, and I had given up all hope of having my wish fulfilled, when one day Dr. Gluck wrote to announce that the operation had been performed, and sent me a photograph of the resulting aspect of the panel, warning me that, while it was no longer daubed over, the cleaning had revealed that the flesh parts were in a poor state, the head of the Madonna having lost some of its glazes. My expectation, however, had been more than realized, and the Vienna picture proved to be a fragment of a larger work. Freed from the repainting that had deliberately covered it up, there appeared below to our left two hands holding a glass filled with a liquid. The hands postulated a figure, that figure postulates at least one other, and both an altar-piece. This much is settled, but unfortunately I have not been to Vienna since, and it is likely that certain minutiae, and nuances which might affect my judgment escape me. On the other hand, even the photograph reveals that the picture has gained a great deal by its cleaning. The oval of the Virgin's face has come out longer and lost its somewhat vacuous, rustic look. The Child too has grown more alert and alive. The modelling, despite abrasion, has become subtler and more delicate. The line is more vibrant and the edges more crisp. We can no longer mistake it for the effort of a provincial. It is the achievement of an artist. Who he was will be discussed in the following pages.

* * * * *

Viewed in the light of all that we have come to know about Antonello, the Vienna "Madonna" belongs so manifestly to his circle that there is no room for doubt. The only question is whether it was painted by the master himself or by a follower; and in order to answer it, we must make investigations. In the first place, we shall examine the internal evidence and see whether the panel could have been painted by Antonello. Then we must make sure that no other artist is so likely to have done it. After this we shall study the texts that speak of the S. Cassiano altar-piece, and decide whether our Madonna could have formed part of it. Finally, if the Vienna "Madonna" formed part of an altar-piece which necessarily exerted considerable influence, we should expect to discover and must look for traces of it in works painted during the years that followed Antonello's sojourn in Venice.

* * * * *

In the first place, then, let us examine carefully and minutely the Vienna "Madonna" and see whether she has the characteristics, qualities, and peculiarities of an autograph work by Antonello.

She is seated almost frontally against a creased curtain, between the high arms of a box-like throne, with her feet resting on a flat cushion. The palm of her hollow right hand holds cherries, while her left rests on the shoulder of the Holy Child, Who sits in her lap blessing with His right hand while His left holds a book open on His knee. Both Mother and Child look with wide-open eyes out of the picture, she pensively, He more eagerly. Their mouths are slightly open, His as if speaking, hers as if about to speak. At the bottom of the panel to our left appear two hands, the right supporting and the left grasping a glass.

When attempting to discover the author of an unknown work we instinctively look first at the faces. I am not sure that in our picture they would instantly have suggested Antonello. This is not surprising, for this artist had no constantly recurring facial type. You will find no two ovals that closely resemble each other. Our Madonna has a certain likeness to the one in the Antwerp "Crucifixion," and to the Dresden "Sebastian" as well, less naturalistic than the first, less conventional than the second; but it is not on such evidence alone that one would be satisfied to base an attribution. Nor need we, for happily there is no lack of other and more convincing testimony.

Much more characteristic of Antonello than everything else is the tendency of his design to approach the geometrical forms that would most closely embrace the shapes he has to represent. In this case a tall pyramid would comprise the whole group, and a shorter truncated one the lap and extremities of the Virgin. Without in the least suggesting the barbarously crude sacrifice of naturalness, comeliness, and seemliness to geometrical obviousness practised by our recent Cubists during their brief moment of vogue, the designer of this pattern converges all his lines upon this effect. In so far as compatible with the needs of representation, they tend downward until, when these have well established the general form of the tall pyramid, other lines more or less horizontal build up the base. Hence that peculiar system of folds covering knees and feet which was so often imitated by Antonello's followers. But as general design, which is so much more an affair of the head than of the hand, is what intelligent followers imitate easiest and best, it remains to be seen whether in the absence of exact parallels among Antonello's autograph paintings, this solution of the problem of geometrical representation is only good enough for them, or so much better than theirs, that it must be his own. We shall, however, defer this inquiry for the moment, for it will find its answer in the next section, and we must devote the rest of this one to the study of more specific evidence.

Drapery is the chief means by which a design like this of ours is realized, and drapery in turn is largely a matter of tissue and folds. Here there is nothing in tissue that is unlike or unworthy of Antonello, and in the folds there are such identities of peculiarity and quality that it would be startling if they were not by him. The patterns of the brocades have every resemblance to those in works as indisputable as the Messina Polyptych and the Syracuse "Annunciation." The folds beginning with the crease in the curtain (as in all his *cartoline* bearing signatures) and ending with the toss of the dress over the flat pillow almost exactly as in the Madonna of the Antwerp "Crucifixion," have the loops, and edges, and crispness found in all his authentic paintings. In the main, however, they show almost the geometrical tendency of those in the figure of the Virgin at Syracuse, relieved, as there, by the bulge of the vertical drapery over the chest. The lines in the kerchief under her throat have the exact movement and quality of those in the linen visible over the angel's collar in the same "Annunciation." Even such a casual matter as the tossing to one side of the lower part of the curtain is paralleled in the background of that picture. If I chose to make comparisons with works not yet universally accepted as Antonello's, as for instance Mr. Benson's "Madonna," I could find further striking resemblances; but I deliberately look for them in such paintings alone as signatures or documents and internal evidence combine to put beyond question.

Hands are if anything even more peculiar to the artist than folds. The two in the lower left-hand corner holding the glass are so entirely in the scheme of hands like the Angel's at Syracuse and the Madonna's at Messina that they alone would suffice to make me wonder whether the work in which they occurred was not by Antonello. The right hand holding the cherries has the thumb firmly bent back as in the Messina Madonna just mentioned, and the Virgin in the Syracuse "Annunciation" once again. As for the other hand in our picture it is singularly like that of the Gregory in the Messina Polyptych.

ANTONELLO DA MESSINA

[*Syracuse.*

ANNUNCIATIO

Even such trifles as the billets and circlets embellishing the throne re-occur in the Syracuse picture, besides a bit of carving so lingeringly Gothic as the kind of quatrefoil that we get a glimpse of on the seat.

We agreed that there was no great likeness in type between the two faces in this picture and others of Antonello's. Yet when we turn our attention to details there is no lack of resemblances. Thus the modelling of the mouth and chin of the Child recalls the Dresden "St. Sebastian," and the Virgin's mouth if closed would resemble more than one in Antonello's portraits. Finally, the hair of the Child, with its rebellious curls, is painted with a vividness of touch that reminds us of the Gabriel at Syracuse.

The design and peculiarities of the Vienna "Madonna" thus point to Antonello as its author, and it now remains to be seen whether anything is hidden away in this panel that betrays a later date than 1479, the year of Antonello's death, and then to inquire whether as an artistic achievement it has his quality.

Search as I would, I have found no trace of anything that must have been done after 1479. On the contrary, there is good reason for assuming that it was probably designed three or four years earlier. The Virgin's oval reminded us of the one in the Antwerp "Crucifixion." That painting is dated 1475. Its background represents the Straits of Messina, and in the figures I discover nothing that its painter need have borrowed from Venice. It is not improbable, therefore, that this masterpiece was painted early in that year before he left home. At the same time the Virgin's oval is well on the way toward the more conventionalized one of the Dresden "St.

Sebastian." The exact date of that noble work must be ascertained on internal evidence. How late it is we are not called upon for our purpose to discuss at length, although for the benefit of those who wish for my opinion I venture to say that in all probability it was painted before Antonello left Venice and therefore in 1476. But one fact is clear, that it could not have been designed before its author had had time to become saturated with Venice, and acquainted with Mantegna's frescoes at Padua—an acquaintance he easily might have acquired on his way to and from Milan in 1476. We conclude therefore that the oval alone of the Vienna "Madonna" would make us date the picture between early in 1475 and somewhere in 1476. Other considerations confirm this dating but incline one to approach it to the earlier, rather than to the later work. We discovered in the course of our examination that no morphological or other details here but reminded us of the Messina polyptych of 1473 and of the Syracuse "Annunciation" of 1474. Now it appears clearly enough in the Dresden "St. Sebastian" that Venice and Lombardy purged Antonello clean of all Gothic fossilizations. If they still lurk in our Madonna it can only be because he designed her soon after he reached Venice. We need not discuss whether it might have been painted earlier as it is not a question likely to be asked by serious critics.[1] We may thus safely assume as highly probable that our Madonna was designed in 1475, and we shall see later that the acquisition of this point is of some importance.

[1] The oval of the Madonna and the type and action of the Child are like enough to faces and figures designed by Bellini toward 1475 to make it probable that they already witness to the influence the Venetian exerted upon the Sicilian.

ANTONELLO DA MESSINA

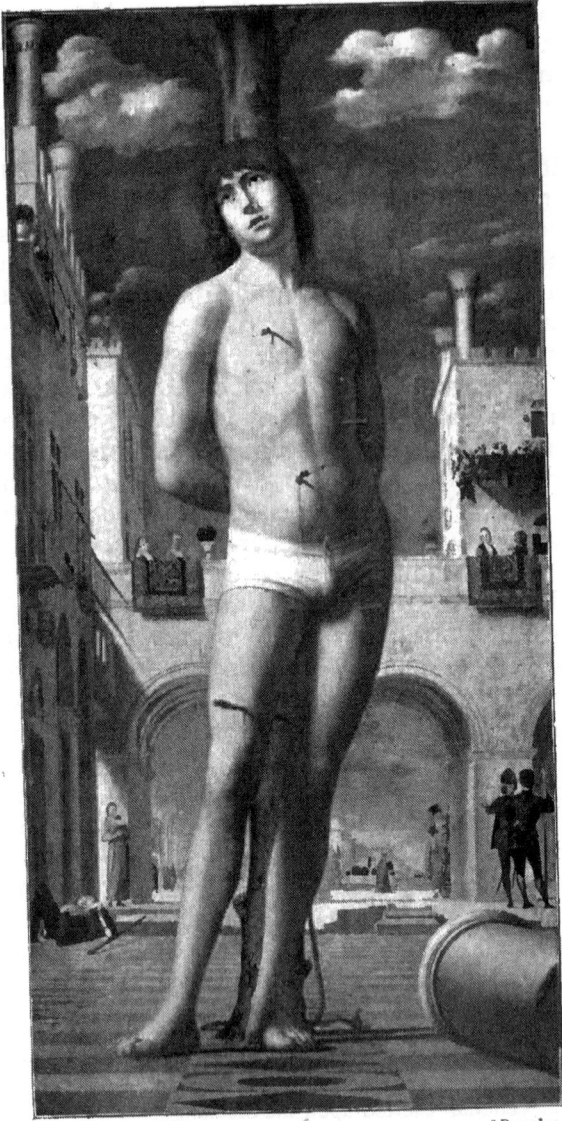

[Dresden.

ST. SEBASTIAN

If we pass outside these questions of morphology and chronology we shall find nothing in the Vienna Madonna that forbids our attributing her to Antonello. Nor in the quality either is there, in my opinion, anything to prevent our confirming this view. Allowing for abrasion and the loss of glazes, I find the modelling of the flesh parts good enough for any of the greater Quattrocento Italians, and surely not unworthy of Antonello. It has his large simple planes, his breadth, and his solidity, as they occur in the precise stage of his evolution that we should expect in a work executed between his Syracuse "Annunciation" and the Dresden "St. Sebastian." The draperies are as logical and well arranged as in any of his works, and I find the kerchief remarkable in the way it helps us realize the volume and weight of the Virgin's head. Nor can I discover anything in the draughtsmanship that Antonello need disown.

As appreciation is a subject for rhetoric rather than demonstration, I will say no more on this point, but appeal to the student to look well and sympathetically before he decides to be of a different opinion.

* * * * *

This ends our first inquiry, namely as to whether the internal evidence permits us to believe that Antonello could have painted our picture. The answer is favourable. We now proceed to make the second which is whether any other artist is as likely to be its author.

In order to attain this end we are scarcely called upon to go through the whole list of Italian, or even Venetian painters. All but a few we can eliminate at once as unlikely to have designed our picture.

Those few will naturally comprise first and foremost Antonello's own family and other Sicilians, then some of his followers in Venice, and finally artists like Boccaccino, the Pseudo-Boccaccino and Fogolino who have been named as its possible authors.

I shall not attempt to give an account here of Antonello's son, nephews and Sicilian followers, as this has been done with ample bibliographies and adequate illustrations by Professor Venturi in vol. vii, part iv of his indispensable "Storia dell'Arte Italiana." It is perhaps unfortunate that of Antonello's son, Jacopo, only one known work now remains. That one, the Bergamo "Madonna" was painted in 1490, eleven years after its author, upon his father's death, was left to complete his unfinished commissions. He thus evidently succeeded to the studio and traditions, but this one remaining work proves that he did not succeed to his father's genius. For the Bergamo "Madonna" is an artistic achievement of quite subordinate interest and small aesthetic merit, and it is not easily conceivable that the man who painted it at the age of thirty-five, when he should have been doing his best, had ever done better. Of the father's genius there is no trace, and all his peculiarities and predilections as of type, and pose, and system of folds are reduced to silly, niggling mannerisms. Jacopo's modelling is bumpy and hard with a dizzy confusion of planes, his drawing contemptible, his draperies unfunctional, his feeling mawkish. It is only fair to invite comparison of the Child in his Bergamo panel with the one in the Vienna "Madonna," for the first is little else than the other reversed. I do not fear that any serious critic will allow that the painter of the Child in the one, with the silly head, wretchedly drawn limbs, and meaningless draperies could also have painted the

ANTONIA DE SALIBA

[Spoleto.

MADONNA ENTHRONED

other. The relation is too obviously that of a brainless copy to a creation.

Antonello's best known Sicilian follower was his own nephew Antonio de Saliba. Although he was the pupil of his cousin Jacopo, we should never suspect it, for, either because Jacopo himself was merely a copyist of his father, or because his own efforts could not so much as attract an apprentice's admiration, Antonio betrays no manifest signs of dependence on Jacopo, but imitates closely his great namesake. Much of the confusion, by the way, which has reigned hitherto with regard to the great Sicilian was due to the fact that in signing both called themselves by the same name. Happily documents have helped to clear up the confusion which Morelli's discerning eye for quality had already nearly achieved, and there is no further reason for failing to distinguish between them.

I believe I am fairly well acquainted with this modest artist. I have traced all the works ascribed to him in Sicily and Calabria, and I have seen everything passing or likely to pass under his name in the rest of Europe and in America. I do not hesitate to say that he never gives sign of the mastery and art revealed in the Vienna "Madonna." Luckily we have the means of making a most striking comparison. On his way between Sicily and Venice he painted for an Umbrian mountain village a picture which some years ago was brought down to Spoleto and thus made accessible. In a frame of the period we see the Madonna enthroned, and above in the lunette, the Eternal between cherubim. He concerns us to the extent only of showing what a mediocre artist the author was, but the Madonna was obviously painted by a man whose mind had retained a most vivid imprint of our Madonna or another of all but the same design. Now every difference in the mere pattern might be explained away by a difference in date. Thus it is conceivable that the broader throne, and the more free toss of the draperies were due to a later and looser phase of the same career. It is perhaps conceivable too, although less likely, that the creator of a volume so deliberately pyramidal or conical as the mass of the Vienna " Madonna" would have forgotten his own instincts to the extent of giving the Virgin a somewhat shrinking action of the torso, in contradiction with its ideal geometrical envelope. But what I cannot conceive is that the artist who once had risen to the artistic quality of the one should have declined to the other with its heavy shadows, dryness, paperiness, and thin, jejune effect.

I cannot believe in such a decline; and to me it is evident that the author of the Spoleto picture could not have been the author of our Madonna. Similar reasons will not allow me to believe that the painter of ours could have fallen to the level of painting the Madonna belonging to Baron Corrado Arezzo at Regusa Inferiore in Sicily (Venturi's "Storia," vii, 4, p. 83), or the Madonna belonging to Mr. Grenville L. Winthrop of New York (Berenson, "Venetian Painting in America," Fig. 20), both better than the Spoleto one, but far inferior to ours, both works that I am inclined to ascribe to the earliest years of Antonio de Saliba's career. If the " Madonna del Rosario " at Messina is not by the same, but a different author, his work is every bit as inferior to ours. Salvo d'Antonio is not more likely to have designed our Madonna than Piero da Messina, for the first in his one known work, the " Dormition of the Virgin," formerly in the Cathedral of Messina, is at once Carpacciesque, Umbrian and poor, while the second was even below the level of his brother, Antonio de Saliba, whose pupil and imitator he seems to have been. There remain three other Sicilian pictures whose authors we may mention here. One is the panel in the Cathedral at Syracuse where we see the Madonna enthroned with two angels blowing trumpets (Venturi, "Storia," vii, 4, p. 82). It is a rather attractive work, later I should say than ours, but with more Gothic reminiscences. Its painter's intimate qualities of drawing and modelling are, however, at least as bad as Antonio de Saliba's. The other two pictures are the "Madonna" in the Salting Bequest of the National Gallery and the "Female Saint" in the Walters Collection at Baltimore (Berenson, "Venetian Painting in America," Figs. 18 and 19). Their author was indeed a much worthier follower of the great Antonello than any other of the Sicilian artists known to us, but not only is he distinct in character, but incapable, I believe, of having created the "Madonna" at Vienna.

I do not fear that the student who has given his careful attention to the Sicilian painters I have just enumerated will dissent from me and conclude that any of them might have created a masterpiece like our Madonna. In Venice there were of course artists who had genius enough for such an effort. The Bellini, Montagna, or Cima would perhaps not have been baffled to achieve a work of as high a quality, but we know them well enough to feel confident that no product of their art would have had this exact character. People, however, of the stamp of Alvise Vivarini, Cristofano Caselli, Filippo Mazzola, Lazaro Bastiani or Benedetto Diana, all of whom imitated Antonello, were never capable of such a creation. It would be tedious and useless to discuss this statement which must seem fairly credible to all who have a sufficient acquaintance with these painters. So we shall now attend for a moment to the claims of Boccaccino, the Pseudo-Boccaccino, and Fogolino, not that these are in any way more justifiable than others, but because they have got into print, the first through Wickhoff, the second through myself, and the other through Professor Venturi.

Now that Antonello is better known to us, and in phases related to this picture, the claims of these painters are no longer worth serious discussion. Boccaccino, it is true, constantly has, as we said early in this essay, the round wide-open eyes of our Madonna and an oval recalling hers. He also has a liking for the same sloping silhouette of the shoulders, and the vertical rhomboid fold over the right hand. He affects rich stuffs as well, and I recollect one instance where he has a thumb pushed back as Antonello has it.[1] All of which means simply that Boccaccino was well acquainted with either our "Madonna" or another very much like it. In their intimate nature, however, there is nothing in common between his art and that revealed in the picture at Vienna.

Ten years ago, when I ventured upon the guess that he might have painted this work, the Pseudo-Boccaccino was an artistic personality that seemed to hold out promise. I had not seen the Vienna picture for many years, and did not even possess a reproduction of it. In the light, however, of all that we have learned since about Giovanni Agostino da Lodi (the real name of the "Pseudo-Boccaccino"), the

---

[1] It occurs in a Madonna in the collection of the late Theo. M. Davis which bears a more than accidental resemblance to the upper part of the Antonellesque "Madonna" in the Syracuse cathedral referred to a page or two ago (Photo Alinari 33342).

MARCELLO FOGOLINO

MADONNA AND SAINTS

attribution to him of such a masterpiece has become little less than absurd, despite the justification offered by certain Antonellesque details of arrangement and folds in such typical works in and near Venice as the "Youthful Christ between two Apostles" of the Academy, the "Marriage of St. Catherine" at S. Stefano, and the altar-piece at S. Pietro in Murano. These in their turn do in fact indicate that their author was acquainted with our "Madonna" or another almost identical with it, but give ground for no further inference than that.

Professor Adolfo Venturi's attribution [1] to Marcello Fogolino, the puffy, empty, crude provincial, would be quite unintelligible but for the probability that the critic was subconsciously influenced by the Benson "Madonna," which used to pass as Fogolino's (although by Antonello, as I am convinced), and also for the fact that the same Fogolino all but copied our "Madonna" in his Hague altar-piece. I get the impression, however, that Professor Venturi will not insist on his attribution, seeing that he is at the pains to add that the Vienna picture is "rendered with such fidelity to Antonellesque peculiarities as to lead us to regard it as an imitation of a lost original by the master of Messina."

* * * *

Hitherto I have tried to establish, in the first place, that the Vienna "Madonna" contains nothing, whether as character or quality, peculiarities or date, that need make us hesitate long in ascribing it to Antonello, and then that no other artist known to us can establish claims at all so well founded. Let us now see whether the information handed down to us regarding Antonello's S. Cassiano altar-piece

[1] "Storia dell' Arte Italiana," vii, 4, p. 648

allows us to conclude that our panel, which, as we have not forgotten, is only a fragment, originally formed part of it.

It turns out that we know very little about that altar-piece, famous as it was. As so often happens, contemporaries saw no need of describing the evident and familiar, and they omitted to record just how many and what figures this master-piece contained and how they were related to one another. Marino Sanuto speaks in 1493 of "several saints"—*alcuni santi*—and Ridolfi in 1648 adds that one of them was a Michael. But as Ridolfi tells us that in his day the altar-piece had already disappeared he was perhaps speaking from hearsay only. Not another word about the composition of the design is known to be in existence, but happily a document found years ago by Senator Beltrami gives us the exact date of the work. It was begun in August 1475 and on 16 March of the following year was within twenty days of completion.[1] The other references to the altar-piece are laudatory. The Venetian nobleman, Pietro Bono, who ordered it, writes to the Duke of Milan that when finished, "it will be one of the finest works of painting in or out of Italy." Matteo Colaccio in 1486 finds it worthy of the greatest admiration. Sabellico toward 1492 remarks that in the S. Cassiano altar-piece Antonello shows that there is nothing he cannot paint with the exception of the soul. Marino Sanuto in 1493 observes in accord with the last writer that the figures in this picture seem alive and want nothing but soul.

[1] The data will be found resumed with his usual clearness and accuracy by Dr. Gronau in the "Repertorium," xx, p. 347, *et seq.*, and more briefly in both the Venturis, in the notes by Dr. Borenius to the new edition of Crowe and Cavalcaselle and in Dr. von Hadeln's notes to his edition of Ridolfi.

We gather, therefore, that Antonello's S. Cassiano altar-piece consisted of a Madonna with several saints, one of whom was Michael, that it was begun in August 1475, that it excited great admiration, but that it already struck spectators in less than twenty years after its completion as rather expressionless—" without soul." Singular by the way, and most interesting this craving for soul suddenly appearing between 1486, when Colaccio does not miss it, and 1492, and 1493, when Sabellico and Sanuto cry for it.

Now there is nothing in all this to veto the acceptance of the Vienna " Madonna " as the central part of the lost S. Cassiano altar-piece. The two hands holding a glass that peep out of the lower left hand corner bear witness to the fact that they must have belonged to the figure of a saint standing almost in profile to our right.[1] Analogy leads us to expect another female saint nearly facing her on the other side. Each of them, if the altar-piece had four saints, one of whom was Michael, would have been flanked by a male saint, seen probably more frontally. Such a reconstruction would have nothing that was not customary in the arrangement of a Quattrocento altar-piece, and the S. Cassiano one necessarily must have had such a disposition.

The only consideration which at this point could prevent our accepting this Vienna " Madonna " for the central fragment of the lost altar-piece would be

[1] The identification of this saint might contribute something to the solution of the problem, but I can find no clue to it. In the Bergamo Gallery there is a panel ascribed to G. da S. Croce but more likely by Cristofano da Parma, in which, too, there occurs a female saint holding a glass half full of a liquid, and a palm. The saint occurs again in Alvise's earlier altar-piece at Berlin. In both galleries she is designated as the Magdalen, but the palm of martyrdom does not belong to Mary of Magdala.

if the known date of the latter did not harmonize with the chronology of the Vienna panel as ascertained from internal evidence. There is, however, no clash. On the contrary, the chronology which we examined exhaustively in its place led us to conclude that, if by Antonello at all, the panel must have been designed between the Antwerp "Crucifixion," dated 1475, and the Dresden "St. Sebastian," painted most probably in 1476. It appeared, further, that owing to the lingering in our picture of certain Gothic touches, like those in the Syracuse "Annunciation," it is more likely to have been painted in the earlier rather than the later part of Antonello's sojourn in Venice. In sober truth the history of art could not show many instances in which the results of internal evidence were in such complete agreement with the documentary facts.

Meagre as the descriptions of the S. Cassiano altar-piece are, on one important matter they give us very interesting information, namely, that, as we have seen, it was lacking in soul. Now "soul" has for the time being fled from our tongues and our lips, and retreated to the inner chambers of our heart, where it abides in safety, unseen and unheard, until hell and all its hosts shall have ceased holding high carnival on the face of this once fair earth. But in people of my generation the demand for soul was clamorous, and even those of us who were aware that it was absurd to expect its special manifestations anywhere and everywhere, wistfully missed it and could scarcely surrender themselves to a work of art that was without it. The almost total absence of soul probably prevented our grasping the importance of the Vienna "Madonna," which lacks it quite as much as Sabellico and Martin Sanuto found it lacking in the San Cassiano altar-piece.

I suspect that those humanists of four centuries ago when they used the word soul really meant to speak as we still do of emotional expression of an elevated and elevating order. It is true that our younger generation—that is to say the part of them that makes itself heard—has turned away with nausea from that kind of expression, but only because it craves in turn for an opposite kind of expression: the expression of sneering scorn, greedy revolt, base resentment, and ignorant pride.

But the Vienna "Madonna" makes no appeal of any kind. Its business is to exist, and like the creations of most other impersonal, impassive, disinterested artists, of Piero della Francesco, Paul Veronese, and Velasquez for instance, it is no incarnate symbol, and has no message. Its sheer existence is life-enhancing.

For these reasons I fear that the student may at first be disappointed in this work. Despite his acquaintance with Antonello, than whom, let us bear in mind, there has been no artist less emotional, less rhetorical, less appealing, he probably has been expecting of an epoch-making masterpiece by a great artist something sublime and exalted. At least I did, and it took me a long time to yield to the evidence and to recognize that this "Madonna" not only must be by Antonello, because it had his character and his quality, but was worthy of having formed the central part of his famous altar-piece. Of course it has lost much from both the neglect and attentions of men and not a little from the tooth of time, but it loses much more still from having been torn out of its context, so to speak, where, as a figure enthroned high over other figures, it may have produced a more arresting, a more commanding impression.

It should be remembered, furthermore, that it was

admired probably for novelties of technique and design as much as for aesthetic reasons. The first now escape us almost altogether, and the second largely, for the admiration was not lavished of course upon the fragment now present, but on the entire composition. If imitation is the test of admiration we shall presently find ample proof that our "Madonna" was much admired.[1]

* * * *

Let us see what point we have reached. In the first place we investigated the internal evidence and concluded that morphology, chronology, and quality all permitted us to believe that the Vienna "Madonna" was by Antonello. Then we took pains to make sure to the best of our ability that no other artist could have designed her. Finally, we studied the documentary and literary references to the S. Cassiano altar-piece, and concluded that our "Madonna" most probably formed part of it.

To clench the argument we must now proceed further and make the fourth and last inquiry, namely, this. If the Vienna "Madonna" formed part of an altar-piece which necessarily exerted considerable influence, we ought to find traces of it in the works of artists painted in the years that followed Antonello's sojourn in Venice.

We have already had occasion to look at pictures by the pseudo-Boccaccino, Boccaccio Boccaccino, and

[1] The S. Cassiano altar-piece may have been removed because it had become unpalatable to Seicento taste with its craving for theatrical appeal, and the patrons of the chapel were rich enough to replace it. Agents of foreign collectors may have thought less ill of it; but unable to transport the whole, carved out the Madonna alone. It is not inconceivable that other fragments may turn up or be identified.

Marcello Fogolino, painted through the entire first quarter of the sixteenth century, in which traces of the imitation of our "Madonna" were perceptible, palpable, or obvious. I suspect we could find down to the middle of the sixteenth century such witness to the immense hold this work took on Venetian painting. It is much more interesting, however, to see how it affected more important men who happened to be closer contemporaries. We begin with the greatest figure in Quattrocento Venice, Giovanni Bellini.

We shall not expect him to imitate anyone or anything crudely or obviously. Plebeian gossip accused him of stealing Antonello's technical processes rather than his design. With the question of oil painting in Venice we are not here concerned, although it is not to be questioned that the Sicilian's sojourn there encouraged its study and employment. Yet from about 1480, for some ten or fifteen years on, there appears in Giovanni Bellini's works a tendency to give the "Madonna" a conical or pyramidal shape which is never seen in his paintings prior to Antonello's Venetian visit. Up to that date his Virgins have rather square shoulders, heads clearly detached, and arms arranged with no reference to a geometrical shape. After that date head and torso are so draped as to run them into one mass. Conspicuous instances of this new pattern are the Madonnas in the famous S. Giobbe altar-piece[1] of about 1480, the Murano one of 1487, and the Frari triptych of the same year, not to mention less important designs of the same period. I suspect, however, that if only we had not lost the S. Giovani e Paolo altarpiece painted before 1480 we could lay hands on

[1] All the pictures referred to in the rest of this section are reproduced in Venturi's "Storia," vii, part iv.

even completer proof of the way its author was fascinated by Antonello. It is not inconceivable that the whole of that design was inspired by the S. Cassiano masterpiece of which our "Madonna" is a fragment.

Alvise Vivarini was notoriously the imitator of Antonello, with whose works, in so far as they were to be seen in Venice, he must have made himself perfectly familiar. There can be no question that our "Madonna" was among them. His Barletta "Madonna" of 1483 is in essentials but ours schematized and reversed, holding about the same relation to the original, that a rather poor sepulchral brass might have to the fine statue that inspired it. Not so obvious, yet scarcely more doubtful, are the resemblances between the Vienna figure and the Madonna enthroned in Alvise's Berlin altar-piece of about 1484 or so, his finest achievement—resemblances which extend to the facial oval, to the Child perhaps, and to the throne, but are most unmistakable in the almost parallel square-looped folds over the Virgin's lap and feet. But it took Alvise till toward 1488, and then very likely under the stimulus of Giovanni Bellini, to realize the purpose of a design like that of our "Madonna," and to imitate it as unslavishly but as intelligently as he does in his full-length "Madonna" in S. Giovanni in Bragora at Venice, and a little later in the Vienna "Madonna with the music-making angels."

Another of the Venetians whose earliest works are constantly reminiscent of Antonello was Bartolommeo Montagna. It would perhaps be difficult to prove that when he was designing his earlier important work, the St. Bartolommeo altar-piece for Vicenza, he had our Vienna "Madonna" in mind as well as the one in Bellini's S. Giobbe altar-piece, although

BARTOLOMMEO MONTAGNA

MADONNA (Belluno.

something in her oval, more in the folds over her knees, and even the book in the Child's hands, lead me to regard it as probable. There is no room, however, for any doubt that such a "Madonna" as the one at Belluno (No. 34) is reminiscent of it, as we perceive not only in the deliberately conical mass and in the brocades, but most clearly in the open palm with the stretched thumb. How much this Antonellesque design pleased its author we realize when we see that after some ten years he repeated it with but slight changes in his altar-piece of 1490 for the Certosa at Pavia. This, however, is not the only proof that Montagna was acquainted with our Madonna. Another striking instance is the Virgin with conical and parallel folds in the altar-piece at the Vicenza Gallery, representing the "Madonna with the Baptist and St. Onofrio."

Cima da Conegliano was in some ways the Venetian painter who owed most to Antonello, yet so subtle and pervading was the influence that it is seldom if ever possible in the younger man's extant works to discover trace of obvious borrowing. So we do not expect to find in his paintings patent reminiscences of our "Madonna." And it is not worth while and would be tedious to look for echoes of it in the work of such imitators of imitators as Lazzaro Bastiani, Benedetto Diana, Cristofano da Parma and others. It is more interesting to note that even the Veronese painters betray acquaintance with the S. Cassiano picture, as, for instance, Bonsignori in his earliest work, the S. Paolo altar-piece at Verona; and Francesco Morone in his Berlin "Madonna between Antony Abbot and Paul the Hermit."

Finally, before leaving, but without exhausting our investigation into the influence of the Vienna "Madonna" upon Venetian painting which I have limited strictly to the requirements of our purpose, I invite the student to consult Sect. 5, Chapter V of my "Venetian Painting in America: the Fifteenth Century," where he will find an enumeration of certain traits and peculiarities which Antonello either introduced, or rendered fashionable even though they had been in occasional use previously. Having consulted it let him look and see how many can be traced back to our "Madonna."

* * * *

Our inquiries are now at an end. We have seen that the internal evidence is in favour of the attribution to Antonello da Messina of the Vienna "Madonna" which we have been discussing. We have found no one else at all so likely to have designed her. In consulting the information that has come down to us regarding Antonello's San Cassiano altarpiece, we discovered nothing to prevent our concluding that our "Madonna" was the central portion of that work. And this conclusion is confirmed by the fact that Giovanni Bellini, Alvise Vivarini, and Bartolommeo Montagna, not to mention less important masters, are proved to have been acquainted with this design.

At this point only one retort seems possible. It is that, after all, the Vienna "Madonna" may be only a copy of the central figure of that altar-piece. To which I should reply that no dialectic process can establish the difference between a perfectly faithful copy and an original. The discrimination must eventually be left to one's sense of quality. Mine is convinced that our "Madonna," even when studied in the photograph, reveals the hand of Antonello himself. I cannot admit that it is a copy. Yet if it were no more than a copy, but a faithful one—and that much at least we may regard as proved—the historical interest and importance of this picture is not diminished.

July 1916.

THE ENIGMA OF CARPACCIO'S "GLORY OF ST. URSULA"

With the employment of a more careful chronology than has hitherto been common in our studies, I shall try to make it seem probable that Carpaccio did not paint his "Glory of St. Ursula" in 1491, as signed and dated, but nearly twenty years later. If my conclusions are accepted, we are confronted with an enigma, for the inscription is authentic. I may as well confess, at the start, I am more interested in leading up to the enigma than in solving it, although I may venture upon a solution. My real aim, however, is to promote a state of mind that will hesitate to accept documentary or even epigraphic evidence, with regard to a work of art, without first criticizing it in the light of all that can be learnt from the internal testimony of the work itself.

I

Let us see what internal evidence has to say about the "Glory of St. Ursula."

The picture, which hangs in the Venice Academy, is familiar. On a palm tree against the sky, framed in by the mighty arch of an hypaethral structure, stands Ursula in ecstasy, the Eternal hovering over her to bless, naked baby angels crowning her and

VICTOR CARPACCIO

[Academy, Venice.

GLORY OF ST. URSULA

fluttering around her, waving scarves, and a great crowd of worshippers, chiefly women, kneeling at her feet. Above, over the opening in the vault, appear *putti*, who throw down shrubs and flowers. Cherubim form a sort of capital to the trunk of the palm at the point where it begins to burst into foliage.

This work has not had full justice done to it. Its condition is, perhaps, bad and certainly unpleasant, and the device of the tree, be it ever so justifiable symbolically, is visually clumsy and incongruous. There is, however, a further reason, namely, that the whole picture is entirely out of tune with the other scenes of the St. Ursula series. They are gay, lyrically narrative, rich in episode, with a minimum of intellectual design. We are won by their spontaneity and vivacity, and, after revelling in these enchanting qualities, we rather resent the intrusion of a solemn chorale like this " Glory of St. Ursula."

Nevertheless, with the exception always of his highest achievement, the " Presentation of the Holy Child in the Temple," this is Carpaccio's most earnest, most studied, and most impressive composition. Never, with the same exception, does he approach to such gravity of feeling and seriousness of portraiture, to such a concentration and breadth of architectonic design. And yet—how little it amounts to, with every attempt to do it justice! The truth is that, although the artist shows here that he could compose as well as a second-rate Umbrian, it was not what *he* was born to do, and we are not over grateful for the effort. We prefer the boyish, gay, almost frivolous Carpaccio. And here, where we cannot deny a certain seriousness to the design, it is to the sportive *putti* in the vault that our attention more willingly strays.

II

Having looked at the picture, we now can begin to anatomize it with the avowed object of discovering its date. There is no feature, no detail, that may not be useful for this end; but it must be firmly fixed in our minds that the feature or detail which determines the date of a work of art is the latest authentic one. The presence of earlier features may be interesting, and even relevant, but no picture can be earlier than its latest elements.

To begin with the design, I find it too grandiose, and too concentrated for the Carpaccio of the "St. Ursula" series, or even of the S. Giorgio degli Schiavoni canvases. Quite rightly Mr. Roger Fry speaks of the late Carpaccio as more "calculated and harmonious" in his composition, and I venture to believe that the adjectives of the eminent critic apply to our picture better than to any other, excepting always "The Presentation."

The architecture seems more severe, more sober, and more massive than any I can conceive Carpaccio as using during the last decade of the fifteenth century. I feel it to be on the way toward such advanced sixteenth century Venetian building as the interior of S. Salvatore.

The drawing and modelling are not what they are in the rest of the "St. Ursula" series. They are not only unlike, but reveal a difference of purpose and method. In all the canvases of the series except ours, and in all other works more or less of the same period, and indeed for a decade later, Carpaccio draws and models as much as possible like Gentile

Bellini.[1] The effect is linear and even edgy, more, in fact, like Gentile's earliest manner, as manifested in that master's "Beato Lorenzo Giustiniani" than in the same painter's works of the last decade of the Quattrocento. Anyone who will take the trouble to look will be surprised to find how many of Carpaccio's faces of that time are mapped out on the same formula as we note in the Gentile just referred to. In the "Glory of St. Ursula" there is, on the contrary, little line or edge. As in Giovanni Bellini, whose guidance and example its painter is obviously now following, the outline has given way to a contour, which avoids linear effects and reduces to a minimum the use of edge to define the plains within itself. The modelling is obtained by a discreet recourse to a light and shade which are but little contrasted. The purpose is to achieve a head enveloped in atmosphere—as different as possible from the incisive definition taken over from Gentile which characterizes Carpaccio's earlier works. It was while he had this same method in mind that he achieved the masterpiece of his career, the "Presentation of the Holy Child," the treatment of which is, perhaps, the most Bellinesque ever found outside Giovanni Bellini himself. That was in 1510, but Carpaccio could not remain on that pinnacle. The effort must have been too much for him, and apparently it broke him, as a similar effort broke his next-of-kin among Florentines, Andrea del Sarto. By 1515 he had declined to the dryness and smoothness of his "Martyrdom of the Ten Thousand," and, as if to prove that he neither could continue the attempt to rival Bellini nor easily get back to his own nature, he betrays in this wretched

[1] This is the most determining part of the evidence that Gentile and not Lazzaro Sebastiani exerted the chief and vital influence upon the young Carpaccio.

work that he has been imitating the feebler sides of Cima.

The considerations just offered, which would make us date the "Glory of St. Ursula" at about 1510, as well as the first one regarding the architecture and general design, which would fortify this conclusion, are the ones that count most, because, based as they are on feelings of quality and essence, they are the most significant and probing. They are not, however, the most obvious, for the obvious is capable of exact definition and measurement, for which patience, good will, and training suffice; while quality and essence are matters of appreciation, accessible only to a harmony of gifts and culture. Happily more obvious proof that our picture is of about the date of its quality and essence, that is to say of about 1510, is not wanting.

III

Let us begin with the Saint herself. Her attitude and expression represent a state of sentimental ecstasy which is not found in the rest of the "St. Ursula" series, although, in the scenes where she tries to convert her father, in her arrival in Rome, her martyrdom, and her funeral, there was occasion enough for its display, had it been in the artist's mind. At that time it was not in Carpaccio's, nor, indeed, in any other unexpatriated Venetian mind. Sentimentality never reigned in Venice as in the rest of Italy (for which reason, indeed, its art remains so much more palatable through all periods), and the only great Venetian painters through the ages who are tainted with it were Crivelli, Lotto, and Tiepolo, all of whom went from home a great deal, the first two for most

VICTOR CARPACCIO

[Capo d'Istria.

MADONNA AND SAINTS

VICTOR CARPACCIO

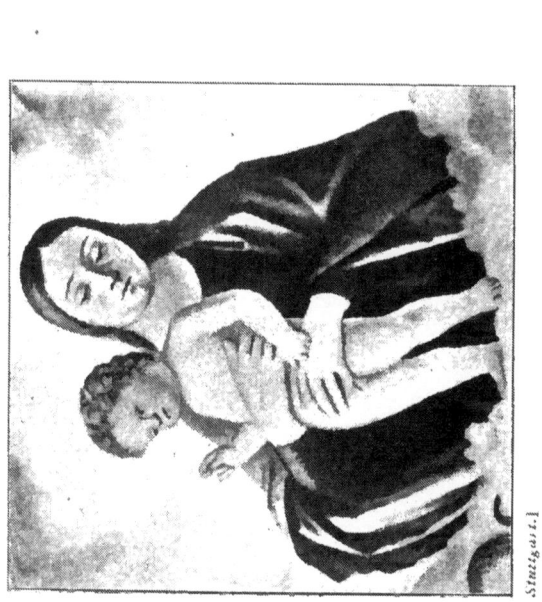

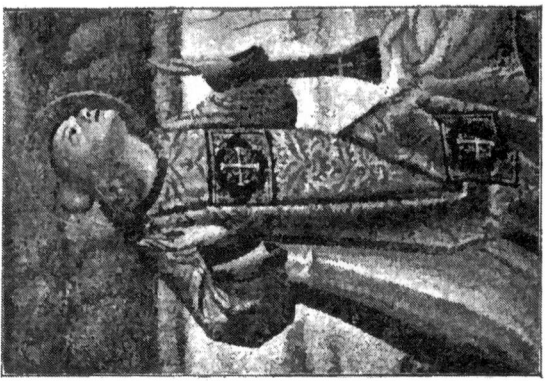

MADONNA
DETAIL.
[Stuttgart.]

ST. STEPHEN
DETAIL.
[Stuttgart.]

VICTOR CARPACCIO

(*S. Giorgio degli Schiavoni, Venice.*)
ST. TRYPHON TAMING A BASILISK
DETAIL

of their lives. For a work done by a Venetian who seldom, if ever, stirred from Venice, this "Glory of St. Ursula," and the Saint in particular, are as sentimental as any we shall find. I venture to maintain that it would have taken a long stretch of years for the author of the boyish, gay, heart-free paintings of the rest of that series to grow into the dangerously close precursor of Guido Reni and his kin that is found here. There is, as yet, but the faintest touch of it in the canvases at St. Giorgio degli Schiavoni, the execution of which must have dragged on from 1502 for nearly ten years. In the latest of them, excepting the "Madonna" over the altar, the one representing "St. Tryphon taming a Basilisk" there is a woman standing near the King with her hands folded in prayer, but without a touch of sentimentality in her face.

And, while we are on this subject, let us glance at the faces of the worshippers. Most of them have a fervour which you will not find in the rest of the series, and some of them as much sentimentality as the Saint herself, and more. A flagrant instance is the pretty young woman on our right, nearly in profile, with elaborate curls, and a throat adorned with a chain and pendant. We find all but the same head, expression, action, and features, on the body of a St. Sebastian in Carpaccio's Capo d'Istria altar-piece painted in 1516. Carried a bit further, we discover it again as St. Stephen in our artist's representation of his martyrdom, now at Stuttgart, painted as late as 1520. Surely if this type of expression had already been used by Victor in 1491, the presumed date of our picture, it could not have failed to appear once in a while during the twenty-five years intervening between 1491 and 1516, when we first meet it again! But I venture to dogmatize and state that, for one possessed with a sense of the organic growth and momentum in the career of an artist and his art, such a head as this in a Carpaccio of 1491 is unthinkable.

Returning to the "St. Ursula," we note that her type of face, with hair parted in the middle and falling without curls or crinkles down the shoulders, occurs in no other work of Carpaccio earlier than the Stuttgart "St. Thomas," dated 1507. The brocade of her mantle is of much larger pattern than in the rest of the series, or than in any of the Schiavoni pictures, and is paralleled only in the brocades found in the "Meeting of Joachim and Anna," of 1515, and the mantle of a spectator on our left in the Louvre "Preaching of Stephen," painted in 1514.

The baby angels playing around her with scarves are nearer in feeling to Correggio and Lotto than to our ordinary notion of Carpaccio. In his works they are paralleled for the first and only time in a frieze below the "Madonna" at the Schiavoni, a work of no earlier date than 1510, and wholly designed, if not entirely executed by Victor.[1] Suggestive, once again, of Correggio and Lotto are the *putti* peering through the roof, and I should not wonder if Lotto had this motive in mind when, in 1513, he began his great altar-piece for S. Bartolommeo at Bergamo. He was not a person to look for ideas in pictures painted twenty and more years ago.

The landscape does not yield much material for our purpose, although some fanciful shapes on the right recall similar elements in Carpaccio's later backgrounds, as, for instance, in that of the "Ten Thousand Martyrs," dated 1515. But the Oriental

[1] In the "St. Thomas" already referred to at Stuttgart dated 1507, instead of a canopy, angels and cherubs stretch and toss a strip of cloth over him like a scarf.

NATIVITY AND DONORS

(Lord Berwick, Atingham (Shropshire).

horsemen who are seen in the middle distance on the left appear in these particular attitudes for the first time in Lord Berwick's "Nativity," in the Schiavoni "Triumph of St. George," and "St. George Baptizing," and in the Correr "Visitation"—all works of about 1508 and later—as well as in the "Ten Thousand Martyrs" of 1515, just referred to.

It now remains for us to examine the worshippers, and see whether they, too, like the rest of this work, suggest many parallels with Carpaccio's later works, and few, if any, with the rest of the "St. Ursula" series. We have already observed that these faces have a fervour and a sentimentality without example in that series, and only to be found in Carpaccio's later and latest works.

Let us suppose for a moment that we did not know when and where and by whom this "Glory of St. Ursula" was painted. Almost the first thing we should do, in order to begin to place it, would be to look at the heads and see what the types, their hair and their costumes told us. Some of the faces here would remind us of Boltraffio, of Granacci, or Ridolfo Ghirlandajo; others, again, of Bartolommeo Veneto, others still of the young Titian, but very few of Carpaccio, the Carpaccio we are most familiar with, the Carpaccio of the "St. Ursula" series. If we ended at last, as it is to be hoped we should, in recognizing this work as his, it would not occur to us to class these heads with his early types, but rather as contemporary with those of the other Cinquecento authors to whom they stand so close.

"Type" and "expression" depend to no slight degree, first on the way of dressing and decking the hair, and then on the rest of the costume. It will be allowed that hair-dressing and costume are a matter of fashion, and very little, if at all, subject to the arbitrament of a portraitist. Even in our days of defiant individualism, revolt against fashion is rare. Four centuries ago it was rarer still. At all events we can safely assume that, if the hair of most of the people in a given work of art is worn in a way that belongs to a definite period of years, and the clothes likewise, the work of art in question must have been created within these years. From this there is no escape, even if some of the figures show traces of earlier fashions.

In our picture a number of the women wear their hair smoothly parted in the middle, and gathered in a flat sort of chignon wrapped in a piece of silk or brocade that encloses it like a bag. They may have elaborate curls at the sides, with or without jewels and pearls as well, or they may not. The point is the chignon.

Well, the first Venetian manifestation of this fashion occurs in the "Doubting Thomas" at Treviso, an altar-piece which many of us believe to be by Sebastiano del Piombo. For our purpose the question of authorship is immaterial, as we are here concerned with the date alone, and that this lies between 1505 and 1506 is established by external evidence. In that picture, however, this fashion is only beginning, while in ours it is already pretty pronounced, nearly if not quite as much as in the marvellous painting in Vienna of a beautiful nude woman, arranging her hair, designed by Giovanni Bellini in 1515.

Considerations of this sort alone compel us to date our picture as somewhere between the two just mentioned, and as not earlier, therefore, than about 1510.

Let us now glance at the three heads of men conspicuous on our extreme left. They remind me ever so much more of Titian in his Pesaro altar-piece than of Carpaccio at any time, and they do not even faintly suggest the author of the rest of the "St. Ursula" series. But, as this statement may be regarded as "subjective," that is to say, the fruit of long-accumulated experience, some may dispute it. For them, too, we have a proof, that is to say, something the first comer can see. The young man in the middle wears the hair over his forehead combed back from the parting in the middle, and tucked behind the ears, while the hair from the crown is brought forward over it and hangs falling to the shoulders. It is a fashion that we shall look for in vain among the bushy, tousled, curly, crinkled heads in Carpaccio's "St. Ursula" series. It is, however, so connected with the Giorgionesque formula that, until recently, its presence was reason enough for ascribing a portrait to Giorgione himself, and, in fact, it occurs in heads like those in Berlin and Budapest, and in the Altman collection in New York, the close relation of which to that master no one will venture to gainsay. That brings us down to a date scarcely earlier than 1505.

There is still more. Among the women on our left, behind the one holding the banner, we see one nearly full face, with marked features and a peculiar head-dress, consisting of a coif floating over the shoulders and gathered up in a noose over the forehead. The almost identical head-gear is worn by the woman already referred to as standing by the King in the Schiavoni "Taming of the Basilisk," a canvas, we said, dating from toward 1510. It should be noted, by the way, that the dress of this woman is singularly like those worn by some of the women in our picture, even to the jewel on the shoulder. In 1907 Sir Sidney Colvin published, in the "Annual of the Prussian Art Collections," a sheet of drawings, with a large head on each side. The one on the reverse is obviously a study for the head that is now occupying our attention, and the other for the woman with the banner. Both were sketches for pose only, and underwent changes, first to give place to portraits, and then because the one with the banner had to be altered from a standing to a kneeling position.[1] But these two drawings happen to have been used by Carpaccio in yet another work, his greatest, the one which, as suggested earlier in this article, our painting approaches closest in artistic and pictorial intention, the "Presentation of the Holy Child in the Temple."

Needless to say that none of these identifications escaped Sir Sidney, nor that there was a discrepancy of nearly twenty years between 1491, the presumptive date of the one, and 1510 the date of the other. He passes it over lightly with the statement that Carpaccio, who made these sketches for the earlier picture used them again for the later.

There are several good reasons why this cannot have been the case. In the first place, there are general considerations derived from the study of drawings. It is my strong impression that a sketch which served for more than one picture was done at a time when all these pictures were already in the author's mind, or on the stocks, or about to follow in close succession. I can recall numbers of such cases in Leonardo and Michelangelo, in Andrea del Sarto and Pontormo, but no exceptions to the rule, although one or two may possibly exist. I refer of

[1] It would seem, therefore, as if the original intention had been to have a group of standing figures representing the Virgins, as in the Brera altar-piece of 1507 by Giovanni Martino da Udine, and that it gave place later to the idea of a crowd of portraits, represented as worshippers, and therefore kneeling.

VICTOR CARPACCIO

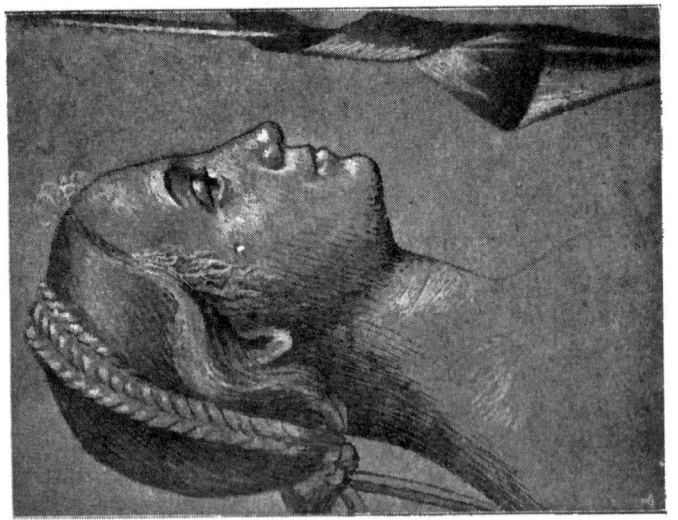

DRAWINGS FOR HEADS

[British Museum, London.

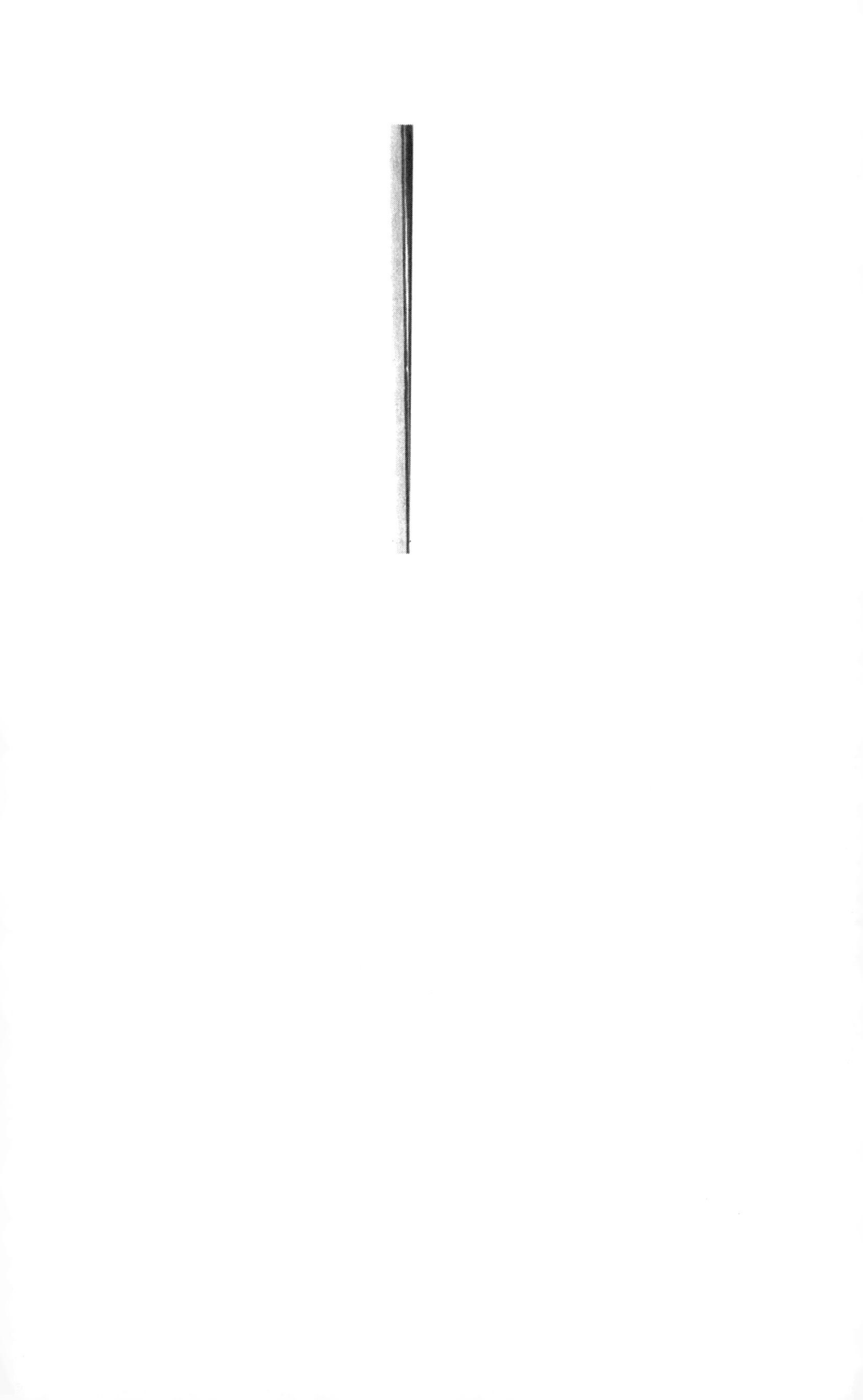

course to the drawings of creative artists, not to those of paste-and-scissors compilers and plagiarists like the Florentine Bacchiacca, and the Venetian Girolamo S. Croce. Then I believe that it could be established that the looser draughtsmanship of the sketches, and better still, the fuller, robuster modelling belong to a much later date in Carpaccio's career than 1491. Finally we return to the fact, so obviously true of the full face, that nothing at all resembling it as head-gear, not to speak of type, occurs any where else in the St. Ursula series. If she reminds us of anything, it is of drawings and paintings by Perugino and Pintoricchio and Raphael, dating from the first years of the Cinquecento. Furthermore, had Carpaccio really made this drawing in 1491, he certainly would have changed it and brought it up to date in 1510. I can recall but two cases in his active career when he all but repeats the same figure. One is the woman with the striped shawl in the "St. George Baptizing" of 1508, whom we find again in the "Consecration of St. Stephen" (now in Berlin) of 1511. Even here, after only three years, the alterations are significant. The other concerns us much more, because one of the figures is King Maurus receiving the ambassadors on their return, one of the St. Ursula series, and its next of kin is the King in the Schiavoni painting representing the "Taming of the Basilisk," which we have already referred to more than once as a work painted toward 1510. Apart from all differences in draughtsmanship and quality, we observe a significant change in head-gear. In the earlier work the King wears a jaunty cap, in the later, the jewelled hat so familiar to us in portaits of the earliest years of the sixteenth century.

At this point I venture to hope that I have brought enough proof to bear to make it certain that our "Glory of St. Ursula" was designed not in 1491, as it is dated, but at a moment only a trifle earlier than the "Presentation of the Holy Child," that is to say about 1510.

IV

If the date is genuine, as we must admit, how shall we account for its being nineteen years out? That is a problem that should have occupied Dr. Ludwig. In his bulky and learned book on Carpaccio he discusses the picture but suspects nothing, so absorbed is he in fitting the portraits with names known to him from documents. Of course he was unaware that names which might conceivably have applied to faces in a work designed in 1491 could not possibly belong to heads painted in 1510. But had the problem existed for Dr. Ludwig, he might well have solved it, for it is one that documents alone will solve to our satisfaction.

I venture to suggest that the date may refer not to the painting of the "Glory of St. Ursula," but to the beginning of the series whereof it formed the central composition.[1] One may then be asked to explain how it is if Carpaccio inscribed the date in 1510 he did not sign, as he invariably did from 1502 on, "Carpathius," but, as in all the other St. Ursula canvases, "Carpatio."

I can only suggest that the artist did so deliberately for uniformity.

October 1915.

[1] I do not forget that the "Arrival at Cologne" is dated 1490, but I adopt Dr. Ludwig's conclusion that it was not painted for the series but anticipated it.

Academy, Venice.]

PRESENTATION OF HOLY CHILD
DETAIL

[Berlin.

MADONNA

A CARPACCIESQUE MADONNA IN BERLIN

This article is about a picture of no intrinsic interest. It will be treated at a certain length, because the discussion will illustrate a point of method vital to the proper pursuit of our studies. The reader who follows me to the end will not, I trust, regret his effort.

I

When the Kaiser Friedrich Museum was inaugurated, a number of pictures that had hitherto been exhibited were removed. The remainder is the result, therefore, of a deliberate selection made for reasons either of aesthetic or historical interest, and it includes a picture (No. 31) which will be the subject of this article.

We see Our Lady sitting in a room by an arched opening which reveals a ravine with a stream running through it, picturesque buildings not far away, and a ridge of hills on the horizon half lost in the mist. She is seen nearly sideways to our left in a somewhat awkward position, absorbed in the book which she holds in her hands, while the Child, reclining precariously on a flat cushion on a narrow ledge, lies asleep before her. The colouring has a certain vivacity, tending to exceeding blondness, and the handling is rather better than the drawing, which, indeed, is not impeccable. The Virgin's knees are a poor affair, and the Child's lower leg would be an unrecognizable object if separated from its foot.

Yet it is a pleasant enough picture. One grasps it easily, for the pattern is large and clear, and the opening on the landscape calls up memories of agreeable experiences, and the dream of enjoying them once more. All the same, one wonders why a work of such modest worth was selected for the brave show of masterpieces decorating the chief Gallery of Germany.

Let us now see what we can get this panel to confess regarding its origin. The impression it makes is that it is very Carpacciesque, but it is not so easy to prove it as I thought. The truth is that a familiarity of many years with the works of a painter ends by giving one an almost instinctive and unreasoned sense of what has affinities or kinship with that painter, which, although at once accurate and reliable, is hard to convey to such as have not gone through the same experience. That of course is why there is so much humbug in our profession, and why it enjoys such a well-earned bad reputation; for not only does it suffer from each honest person's tending to doubt or even deny what has not come into the range of his own knowledge, but much more from the ignorant, the fantastic, and the fraudulent, who cannot easily be brought to book because the evidence concerned is either subjective, or hard to isolate.

But let us make an effort. The oval of the Virgin's face, despite its fullness and heaviness, reminds me of the late Carpaccio, and especially of the large faces in his supreme, although scarcely most characteristic achievement, the "Presentation of the Holy Child in the Temple," a work, as we remember, dated 1510. The nearest likeness, however, occurs

(Comua Hall, Pirano (Istria).

in a painting in the Town Hall of Pirano, dated 1541, and due naturally not to Victor, who was then long dead, but to his son Benedetto. This Benedetto, as all his known authentic paintings tend to establish, did nothing but use and abuse the stock-in-trade and stage properties of his father. Thus, but for the head, the Madonna in his altar-piece is copied from the one in Victor's altar-piece in S. Giorgio degli Schiavoni, while the armoured Knight is taken from an altar-piece of 1518 by his father, which is still to be seen in the Church of St. Francesco at Pirano.

It is by no means unlikely, therefore, that a "Madonna" of this type, created by Victor himself in his later years—that is to say, after 1510—did exist, and inspired the painter of the picture we are studying. Similarly heavy types, with large faces and sleek hair, occur in the "Glory of St. Ursula," the which, although dated 1491, was painted, as I elsewhere have attempted to prove, twenty years later.[1]

The Virgin's hand seems to me very Carpacciesque, but again my impression is not so easy to prove as I had expected, for it is not so much like any one Carpaccio hand as it should be. However, even those severe and sterile connoisseurs who will regard no identity of authorship as proved unless the objects in question would fit accurately into the same mould, will be more ready to accept a less complete resemblance as sufficing to establish a relation of master and pupil, or of their school. The type of hand in our picture, then, occurs from time to time in Carpaccio, as for instance, in the so-called "Courtesans" of the Correr Museum, or in the Berlin "Madonna with Jerome and the Magdalen." Its chief characteristic is the angle formed by the palm

[1] See in this volume "The Enigma of Carpaccio's 'Glory of St. Ursula.'"

and forefinger. This, by the way, I suspect to be a mannerism of Gentile Bellini, for wherever it occurs it can be proved that the painter was a pupil or else close follower of that master.

The folds of the Virgin's sleeves, with loops occasionally flat-ended, are obviously Carpacciesque. The nearest parallel for our picture occurs in that episode of the "St. Ursula" series wherein the Saint attempts to convert her father. As for the rest of the Virgin's raiment, it must be remembered that peculiarities and fopperies of dress are scarcely confined to one artist, and bear clearer witness to the time when a work of art was designed, than to the identity of the designer. The slight variations and additions contributed to current fashion by even so much of a costume painter as Carpaccio, in whom, as in most attractive artists, there was a good dose of the dressmaker, would have been snatched up too quickly by others to admit of their counting as his only.

Turning now to the Child, I am at a loss to find much more to say about Him than that He is decidedly not Quattrocento, but distinctly early Cinquecento, and Giorgionesque rather than Carpacciesque. On the other hand, there is nothing about Him that in the least precludes His having been designed by a close follower of Victor. He is not very different from the Infant in Lord Berwick's "Nativity," and the action and drawing of the legs (although, I grant, it is scarcely a point necessarily significant) recalls the Child of the "Madonna" already referred to at S. Giorgio degli Schiavoni, and in Benedetto's altarpieces. The cushion He lies on is flat, as in the works just mentioned. As for the stepped parapet, that, I suspect, was an invention of Giorgione's. I certainly cannot bring to mind a single instance of it before him.

IN BERLIN

Like the Child, the landscape has a vague, early Cinquecento character, in which there is nothing that a follower of Carpaccio could not have done.

The colouring, as we remember, tends to blondness, in the Child to such excessive blondness as is apt to occur among the Bergamasks who came under the influence of the most eminent of their countrymen, Palma, during his blonde phase. Something, also, in the thick and solid impasto, suggests the same provincials.

II

But for one item of interest, which I purposely defer considering for a moment, our analysis of this panel is now complete, and we can sum up the result.

We cannot reasonably be asked to assign a painter's name to every picture that is submitted to us. The possibility of this is a matter of accident, depending upon whether the work we have studied can be classified with others, of which one at least is known for certain to be by a given painter. The certainty is derived either from an incontrovertibly authentic signature, or from an equally authentic document, on the condition, always, that neither of these be contradicted by the intrinsic facts yielded by analysis of the picture itself. What, in most cases, analysis can and should do is to tell when and where a picture was painted, and to what known following in a school it belongs.

In the case of the picture before us, our conclusions point clearly to Venice, to the close following of Carpaccio, and to the early part of the sixteenth century. To go further, and name the exact date, is doubtless difficult; yet it is of the first importance, in studies of this kind, to narrow, as far as possible, the range of years in which a picture could have been designed.

Although our Virgin is so near to the one of Benedetto's, painted, as we have seen, in 1541, there yet can be no question of this panel being anything like so late, for pattern, drawing, and handling bespeak the severer, stiffer, more restrained craftsmanship practised in the earliest years of the Cinquecento. Earlier than 1500 it cannot be, for the stepped parapet and the Child are Giorgionesque, and we have no Giorgionesque works not by that master himself earlier than the turn of the century. This conclusion is borne out by the embroidery on the Virgin's tunic and its cut, so exactly paralleled in Carpaccio's Berlin picture, which can be of no earlier date than 1505, and in the S. Giorgio degli Schiavoni "Madonna," which could scarcely have been painted before 1510. The Virgin's face, with its heavy mask, recalling the "Presentation of the Holy Child," dated 1510, and the "Glory of St. Ursula," which must have been designed as well as executed at about the same date, are corroborating items.[1]

The net result is that this panel must have been painted by a close follower of Carpaccio at a date scarcely earlier than 1510, possibly in close imitation of a "Madonna" now lost. This follower of Carpaccio, as was almost inevitable at that time, was acquainted with Giorgione's works. If our further

---

[1] This embroidered pattern running down on the tunic from the throat over the chest first occurs, to my knowledge, in the altarpiece of 1505 from Giovanni Bellini's studio formerly in the Ashburnham Collection, and now belonging to Mr. Vernon Watney of Cornbury Park, Charlbury, Oxon.

inference is true, namely that he was a Bergamask knowing Palma in his blonde phase, then we must assume that he painted this panel some years later still, as late at least as 1515, for it is scarcely before this date that Palma's blonde phase would have already attained such a vogue as to produce imitators of it. The Palmesque influence, however, should not be made too much of, for, being confined to the colouring and the handling alone, and not affecting the design or the drawing, its significance is uncertain. It may be accidental, or it may mean—as is more likely—that a young painter who started under the blonde Palma came so recently under the influence of Carpaccio as to lose all that he could of his previous character.

III

Now let us go back and attend to the one item in the panel before us which our analysis has not yet considered. It is a cartel adhering to the raised part of the ledge inscribed with the words "Jacobus Palma", over two crossed palms. "Important, if true," as we say in America.

At Berlin the truth is not doubted and its importance is recognized; and this, indeed, is the reason that the painting, intrinsically so mediocre, was put on exhibition, while many others, as good or better, have been exiled to the provinces or hidden away in store-rooms. The authorities of that wonderful institution, in every re-issue of their catalogue, renew their declaration of faith that our picture is an early Palma. "As an early work this picture suits the character of the master. The influence of Giovanni

Bellini and Carpaccio can still be felt, . . ." says the edition of 1883. "From the master's earliest years," is the brief comment in 1904, and the same words occur in the catalogue of 1909, invaluable for its illustrations. Finally, in the excellent " Guide of the Kaiser Friedrich Museum," issued in 1910, and decorated with a frontispiece representing the subject of the characteristic, the significant, and prophetic controversy over the " Flora," we find the following remarks about our " Madonna": "A work of his first youth reveals the native Bergamask in the direction of Previtali." We may incidentally touch upon some of these highly authoritative statements, but, for the present, it suffices that Berlin official science, for a generation at least, has insisted that the panel we are studying is a very early achievement of Palma Vecchio. Now let us see how it works out.

I quite agree with Berlin that, if the picture were Palma's, it would be a very youthful work. So youthful, indeed, would it be, that years would have elapsed between it and the earliest of those that we usually accept as Palma's first achievements. Otherwise, how account for the almost total absence of any points of resemblance or relation between them? It must date from a time when the artistic personality we call Jacopo Palma had as yet no existence, although the human Giacomo d'Antonio di Nigreti was, no doubt, already alive.

It works out, then, that not earlier than in 1510 Palma Vecchio was still painting in this manner which has so little connection with the first works of his continuous career. For we shall not forget that our analysis yielded 1510 as the earliest probable date, and that the evidence concerned is of a kind that can defy disproval. We shall not forget that, as a Carpacciesque work, its next-of-kin were paintings of Victor's like the Berlin "Madonna with Jerome and Catherine" of a date not earlier than 1505, Lord Berwick's "Nativity," which I suspect is not of that year, but of 1508, and the "St. George Baptizing," which is certainly of 1508, the "Presentation of the Holy Child" of 1510, the "Madonna" at S. Giorgio degli Schiavoni, which is later still, and an altarpiece at Pirano by Benedetto, of 1541. We must not forget that, the sleeveless tunic with its peculiar embroidery does not appear before the Berlin "Madonna with two Saints," and is still found in the Schiavoni "Madonna," while the heavy mask of the face first appears among known Carpaccios in the "Presentation" of 1510. It is most unlikely, therefore, that our panel could have been designed before that date. Furthermore, the colouring, in the Child particularly, led us to suspect that our painter may have got his first training under Palma during Palma's blonde period, and this would bring us down to 1515 at the earliest.

Now we had always supposed that Palma Vecchio was born about 1480, and that he was the pupil of Giovanni Bellini, and the last Berlin Catalogue accepts these data along with the rest of us. But if our analysis of this supposed very earliest effort of Parma's is correct, he was at the very least thirty years old when he achieved it. What is stranger still, the work betrays not the faintest trace of the influence of Giovanni Bellini. On the contrary, the painter appears as a close follower of Carpaccio, and, if any other artist affected him, it was Giorgione, and no older master. But, as Bellini's inspiration is so evident in the Palma that we know, it follows that, if he painted in 1510 at earliest our panel, wherein he is overwhelmingly Carpacciesque and touched by Giorgione, he afterwards put himself so thoroughly at school under Bellini as to lose every remotest suggestion of Carpaccio, and to appear for the rest of his life as the most faithful follower of Bellinesque tradition.

One need not pursue the absurdity further. Had considerations of the kind just brought forward been present in Berlin minds, they doubtless would have thought twice before embarking upon it. But let us now look into the contention of the last Berlin utterance on the subject, namely, that this picture is by Palma because it is "an early work by a young Bergamask in the direction of Previtali." It grieves me to confess that, after poring over it and looking at it from every possible angle and point of view, I still fail to see any resemblance whatever to Previtali in any phase known to me, except, indeed, that this feeble artist imitated Palma as he imitated Lotto, and that a certain tendency to blondness might, perhaps, be regarded as a characteristic of the Cinquecento Bergamasks.

Yet, let us entertain for an instant the idea that this picture was painted by Palma, "a young Bergamask in the direction of Previtali." Presumably, Palma was not more than twenty years old at the time he produced this extremely youthful effort. It was painted, therefore, in 1500. Our first Previtali, however, the Padua "Madonna," is dated 1502, and has no resemblance to our picture in either spirit, design, form or colour, type or treatment. Nor is there any greater resemblance between our panel and Previtali's "Madonnas," in the Budapest, or Pfungst Collections or in the National Gallery, all of them slightly later than the Padua one, nor between ours and the "Madonna between Sebastian and Thomas" of 1506 at Bergamo.

The truth is that in 1500 there were as yet no

IN BERLIN

blonde Bergamasks. It is quite likely that the tendency to this colouring was an idiosyncracy of the one genius of the region, Palma Vecchio himself, and that he imposed it upon his countrymen. I must grant, that the first dated painting in which it appears is not Palma's but Francesco da Santa Croce's "Annunciation" of 1504 at Bergamo, but I believe it is probably only an unhappy accident that we possess no Palma of earlier date in which this tendency might have been anticipated.

* * * * *

"What of the signature?" it may be asked. I said earlier that a signature not only must be "incontrovertibly authentic but must not contradict the facts yielded by analysis." In this case it is in flagrant contradiction with the facts yielded by analysis, and is therefore false—so certainly false that one need speculate no further. The only mention I find of our picture outside of Berlin catalogues is in Crowe and Cavalcaselle who dismiss it with the two words "not genuine." Whether they meant simply that they did not believe it was by Palma, or that it was a forgery does not appear. I scarcely can question that the picture is an old one. The signature may be old too, but not possibly Palma's.

With the claim to be an early Palma, this work loses all interest. I have discussed it at such length in order to be able to point a moral. It is this. There can be no connoisseurship without the most careful and subtle regard to chronology.

October 1915.

GENERAL INDEX

AESTHETIC moment, the, 12, 25.
Analysis, more reliable than documents, 141.
Antonello da Messina, 14, 79-123.
  His influence on Bellini, 75-76, 95-96, 119, 122.
  on Cima, 121.
  on Ercole Roberti, 87.
  on Montagna, 96-96, 120, 122.
  on the "Pseudo-Boccaccino," 113.
  on Alvise Vivarini, 58-60, 120, 122.
Antonio de Saliba, 109-110.
Artistic versus scientific activity, 12.
Attributions, value of correct, 73, 79.

Bacchiacca, 135.
Baldovinetti, Alesso, 26.
Bellini, Gentile, 127, 139-140.
  Master of Carpaccio, 127 n.
Bellini, Giovanni, 38-56.
  His chronology discussed, 55-56, 74-77.
  His development, 48, 49, 75-76.
  His draperies, 51-53.
  Influenced by Antonello, 75-76, 106.

Bellini, Giovanni—*continued*.
  His influence on Carpaccio, 127.
  Influenced by Donatello, 71.
  His modelling, 127.
  His influence on Palma, 145.
  His School, 49, 63-78.
Bellini, Jacopo, 54.
Bartolommeo Veneto and Berlin "Resurrection," 41, 49, and note.
Boccaccio Boccaccino, 98, 112-118.
Boccaccino, Pseudo-, 98, 112-113, 118.
Boltraffio, 6, 20.
Botticelli, 7.
  Compared with Leonardo, 37.

Carpaccio, Benedetto, 139.
Carpaccio, Vittorio, 124-136, 139.
  Follower of, 136-147.
Cézanne, 22, 82, 90.
Chiaroscuro and Contrapposto, 7, 8, 21, 22-23, 25, 27, 28, 30, 31, 32.
Chronology, importance of, 55, 147.
Cima, 48.
  Influence on Carpaccio, 127-128.
Colleoni, Alvise's Portrait of, 58.

149

GENERAL INDEX

Connoisseurship, difficulties of, 138.
Contemporary art, 13, 15, 33, 82.
Crivelli, Carlo, 128.

Donatello, 42, 66, 71.
  His influence on Bellini, 71.
  Donatello and the Vivarini, 72.
Dürer, compared with Leonardo, 37.
Dutch Art, compared with Leonardo's "Benois" Madonna, 28.

Eastern Art, compared with Leonardo, 12-13, 28, 36.
Ercole Roberti, 87.

Fogolino, Marcello, 81, 97 n., 113, 118.
Furtwängler, Adolf, 80.

Gagini, the elder, 83.
Geometrical Design:
  In Antonello, 82-83, 85, 97, 103.
  In Bellini, 119.
  In Cézaine, 82.
  In Giotto, 82.
  In Piero dei Franceschi, 82.
Giampietrino, 20.
Giorgione, xx, 133, 140, 142.
Giotto, 82.
Giovanni Martino da Udine, 134 n.
Greek Art, 33, 36.

Illustration and decoration, 9-10, 13, 14, 15.
Intellectual Art, 27, 31, 33.

Jacopo D'Antonello, 91-95, 108.
Jacopo da Valenza, 61.

Knowing an artist, 42.

Laurana, 83, 90.
Lazzaro Bastiani, 127 n.
Leonardo da Vinci, 1-37.
  Academic interest in him, 21-24.
  Apotheosis of, 17-20.
  Compared with Rembrandt, Dürer, Michelangelo, and Botticelli, 37.
  Drawings of, 26-31, 36.
  His "Leda," 16, 20, 26, 29-30.
  Miscellaneous works attributed to, 19-20.
  Popular works, 20-24.
  Pupils of, 20.
  His "Treatise on Painting," 26.
Lotto, Lorenzo, 40, 128, 130, 146.
Luini, 20.

Mantegna, influence on Antonello, 88, 90, 106.
  Influence on Bellini, 90.
  Influence apparent in Bellini's "St. Justine," 45, 51, 53, 55.
Michelangelo, 28, 31, 32.
  Compared with Leonardo, 37.
Monet, Claude, 26.
Morelli and Morellianism, 34-35, 41, 49, 64, 79, 80.
Mythology, Greek, 15.

Oggiono, Marco, 20.
"Over-meaning" in the work of Art, 10-15, 26.

GENERAL INDEX

Palma Vecchio, 143, 144, 145-146, 147.
Pater, Walter, 2, 3, 14, 20.
Personal equation in Connoisseurship, 63-64.
Physiognomy and "Mona Lisa," 24.
Piero della Francesca, 14, 82, 90.
Predis, Ambrogio da, 20.
Previtali, 146.

Rembrandt, compared with Leonardo, 37.
Romantic movement, 17, 18.

Santacroce, Francesco di Simone da, 147.
Santacroce, Girolamo da, 135.
Sentimentality in Venetian Art, 128-129.
Sketches for pictures as used by artists, 134.
"Soul" in Art, 114-117.

Teniers, 95, 99.

Tiepolo, 128.
Titian, 42.
Type and expression, 131-132.

Uccello, Paolo, 26.

Venice, influence on Antonello, 88.
Vermeer van Delft, compared to Antonello, 90.
Vivarini and Donatello, the, 72.
  School of, 63.
Vivarini, Alvise, 38, 40, 43, 44, 45, 47, 53, 56-61, 62, 63, 64, 65, 70, 71.
  His draperies, 46.
  Inequalities in his work, 43, 44, 57.
  Portraits by, 57-61.
Vivarini, Bartolommeo, 45.

Watteau, compared with Leonardo, 37.
Whistler, 22.

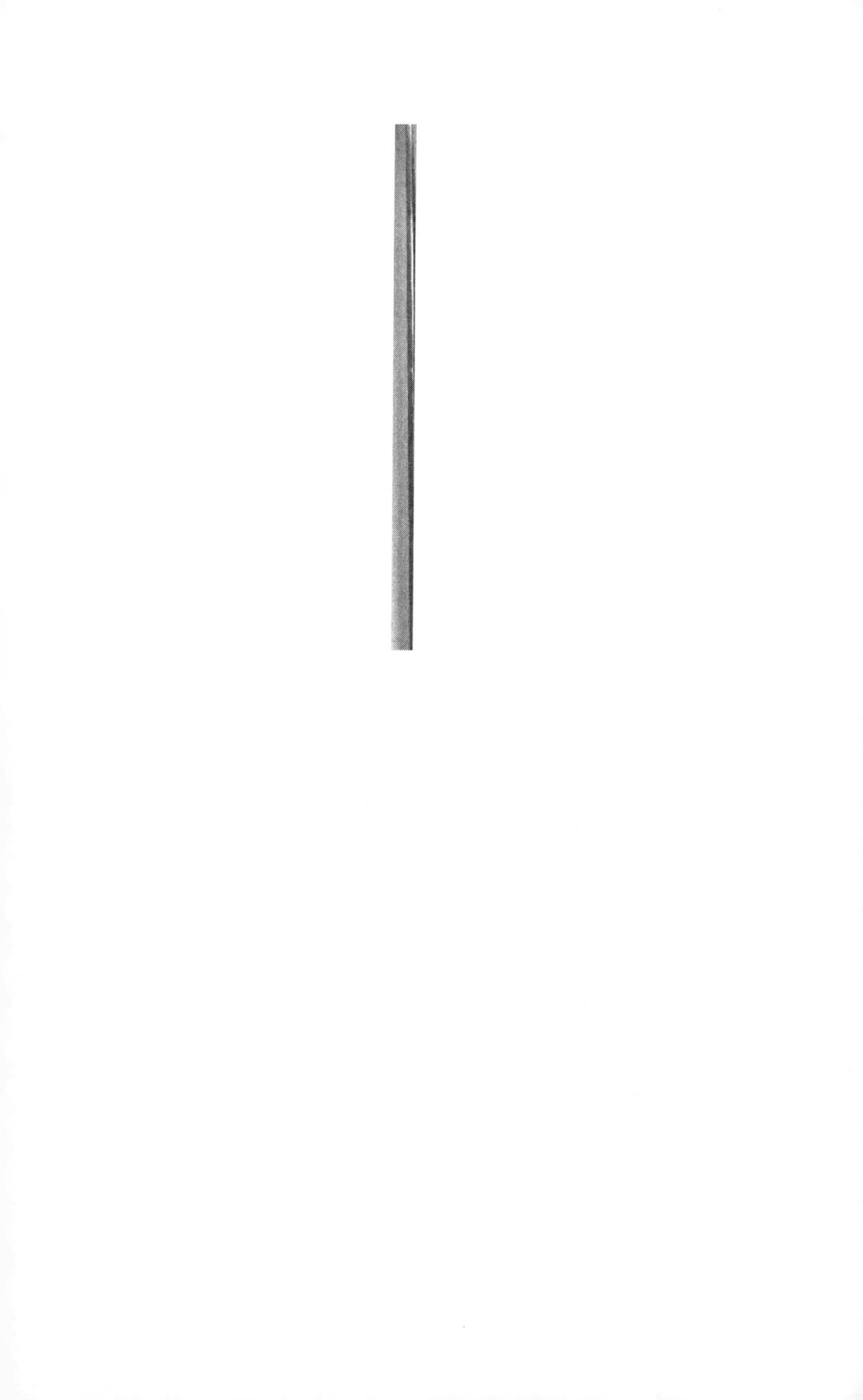

INDEX OF PLACES

ANTWERP: Antonello da Messina, 105.
Ashridge Park (Berkhampstead), Lord Brownlow: Alvise Vivarini, 58.

Baltimore (U.S.A.). Mr. Henry Walters: Palermitan Follower of Antonello, 111.
Barletta, Alvise Vivarini, 43, 57, 61.
Belluno, Bartolommeo Montagna, 96-97.
Bergamo, Giovanni Bellini, 95-96.
    Jacopo d'Antonello, 91-95, 108
    Mantegna, 88.
    Santacroce, Francesco di Simone da, 147.
Bergamo, San Bartolommeo: Lorenzo Lotto, 130.
Berlin: Giovanni Bellini, 42, 49-50 n., 77.
    School of Bellini, 67, 68, 72, 74.
    Correggio, 16.
    Francesco Morone, 121.
    Alvise Vivarini, 46.
    Studio of Alvise Vivarini, 61.
Bologna, Greek Head, 80.
Budapest, Alvise Vivarini, 60-61.
Budapest, Baron Herzog: Alvise Vivarini, 61.

Ceneda (Friuli), Cathedral, Jacopo da Valenza, 61.
Charlbury (Oxon), Cornbury Park, Mr. Vernon Watney: Studio of Giovanni Bellini, 142 n.

Dresden: Antonello da Messina, 105-106.
    Ercole Roberti, 87.
    Giorgione, 79-80.

Florence: Bargello, Donatello, 66, 71.
Florence: Uffizi, Leonardo, 7, 27, 28, 37.
Florence, Mr. Henry White Canon: Copy by Teniers of Antonello, 99-100.
Frankfort a./M. Drawing by Alvise Vivarini, 61.

The Hague: Fogolino, 113.

London, British Museum. Drawings by Leonardo, 27-28.
London, Burlington House. Leonardo Cartoon, 30, 31.
London, National Gallery: Montagna, 97.
    Palermitan Follower of Antonello, 111.
    Alvise Vivarini, 57, 58, 60.

INDEX OF PLACES

London, Wallace Collection: Cima, 48.
London, Mr. Robert Benson: Antonello da Messina, 79-97.
London, former Collection of Sir George Donaldson: Alvise Vivarini, 59.
London, Collection of the late Sir William Farrer: Montagna, 96.
London, Mond Collection: Bellini, Giovanni, 77.
London, Collection of Mr. Fairfax Murray: Alvise Vivarini, 59-60.
Milan, Brera: Giovanni Bellini, 77.
　School of Bellini, 66, 69.
　Giovanni Martino da Udine, 134 *n*.
　Mantegna, 45.
　Alvise Vivarini, 43.
Milan, Bagatti Valsecchi Collection: Giovanni Bellini's "St. Justine," 38-64.
Milan, former Crespi Collection: Giovanni Bellini, 41.
Milan, Cav. Gustavo Frizzoni: Giovanni Bellini, 56.
Milan, Prince Trivulzio: Giovanni Bellini, 41, 49.
Milan, S. Maria delle Grazie: Leonardo's "Last Supper," 1-2, 2, 15, 20, 28-29.
Montefiorentino (Duchy of Urbino): Alvise Vivarini, 45, 63, 72.
Munich: Antonello da Messina, 83, 88.
Münster i./W., School of Bellini, 78 *n*.
Newport (R.I.), Collection of the late Theodore M. Davis: Giovanni Bellini, 41, 49.
New York, Metropolitan Museum: School of Bellini, 78 *n*.
New York, Collection of Mr. Henry Frick: Giovanni Bellini, 49.

Oxford, Ashmolean Museum: Michelangelo, 28.

Padua: Previtali, 146.
　Alvise Vivarini, 57.
Padua, Eremitani: Mantegna's Frescoes, 106.
Palermo: Antonello da Messina, 83, 87, 88, 94.
Paris, Louvre: Giovanni Bellini, 42.
　Leonardo:
　　Annunciation, 7.
　　Belle Ferronière, 6.
　　Drawings, 28, 29.
　　Madonna with St. Anne, 4-5, 20, 26, 30-31.
　　Mona Lisa, 2-4, 14, 20, 2 25, 35.
　　St. John, 5, 14-15, 20, 26, 32.
　　Virgin of the Rocks, 4, 6, 37.
Paris, Collection of Baron Schickler: Alvise Vivarini, 59, 60, 61.
Pesaro: Giovanni Bellini, 77.
Petrograd: Leonardo, 8, 28, 37.
Philadelphia, Collection of Mr. John G. Johnson: Giovanni Bellini, 41, 59.
　Alvise Vivarini, 59.
Pirano (Istria), Town Hall: Benedetto Carpaccio, 139.
Pirano (Istria), San Francesco: Vittorio Carpaccio, 139.

INDEX OF PLACES

Rimini, Town Hall: Giovanni Bellini, 77.
Rome, Vatican: Giovanni Bellini, 49.
Leonardo, 7.
Rome, Minerva: Michelangelo, 32.

Spoleto: Antonio de Saliba, 109-110.
Syracuse (Sicily), Museum: Antonello da Messina, Cathedral, 81.
Sicilian Master, 111.

Venice, Academy: Gentile Bellini, 127.
Giovanni Bellini, Drawings, 51, 52, 56, 70, 77.
School of Bellini, 62-66, 70-74.
Jacopo Bellini, 54.
Carpaccio, 124-136, 138, 142.
Alvise Vivarini, 44, 46, 57.
Venice, Museo Correr: Antonello da Messina, 87.
Giovanni Bellini, 52.
School of Bellini, 66-70, 71, 74.

Venice, Doge's Palace: Giovanni Bellini, 74.
Venice, Giovanelli Palace: Antonello da Messina, 84.
Venice: Church of the Carità, 63, 65.
Venice, Frari: Giovanni Bellini, 44.
Alvise Vivarini, 57.
Venice, San Giovanni in Bragora: Alvise Vivarini, 57.
Venice, Redentore: Alvise Vivarini, 44, 46.
Verona: Giovanni Bellini, 67, 68, 76.
Alvise Vivarini, 43.
Verona, San Paolo: Bonsignori, 121.
Vicenza: Bartolommeo Montagna, 121.
Vienna, Academy: School of Bellini, 66, 68-69.
Alvise Vivarini, 47.
Vienna, Imperial Gallery: Antonello da Messina, 98-123.
Vienna, Baron Tucher: Alvise Vivarini, 59.

Windsor, The Castle: Drawing by Leonardo, 29.

CHISWICK PRESS: CHARLES WHITTINGHAM AND CO.
TOOKS COURT, CHANCERY LANE, LONDON.

Lightning Source UK Ltd.
Milton Keynes UK
UKHW02f1844240918
329461UK00007B/730/P